D1082154

ACKNOWLEDGEMENTS

I wish to thank all the people who helped bring this book to fruition, whether it was through their direct involvement, their encouragement, or their gracious presence in my life.

"The Six P's of Change" would not exist without two people. Period.

Shawn Doyle (www.sldoyle.com) is a talented motivational speaker, author, trainer, consultant and business coach. We have had a mutual admiration society in District 38 of Toastmasters International for several years, competing cordially and then cheering each other on to our subsequent rounds. Shawn had no stake in this book other than the kindness in his heart. Once he knew that I was motivated to write it, he encouraged me, introduced me to printers and potential publishers, advised me on content, and generally gave of his time unselfishly. Shawn, words can never express how indebted I am to you for all that you did. You are a special human being.

Tom Sheehan (www.tomsheehan.com), president of Tom Sheehan Worldwide, became my colleague when he brilliantly collaborated with me to establish global graphic standards for Teleflex Incorporated. When I asked for his advice on publishing my first book, he treated me to a meal and encouraged me to go forward full steam ahead, drawing on his own experience as a producer of his own music. Tom introduced me to editors and weighed in on my designs and other ideas, asking only for an autographed copy of the final product in return. Tom, you will have a copy (actually, probably lots of copies) and my undying gratitude for your generosity of spirit.

Karen McConlogue is more than an editor to me; she became a spiritual life force that guided my creation of this book to its full potential. Karen, when I have time to reflect on the creation of *"The Six P's of Change,"* the most remarkable benefit for me will be that it brought you into my life. I will feel forever blessed for that.

Thom Holden and **Dave Bell**, who are Thom & Dave Marketing Design (www.thomdave.com), made sure that they got the job of designing *"The Six P's of Change"* simply because they wanted to be part of it. Guys, I am overwhelmed with pride by your confidence and your engagement in this book.

Joel and **Andie Garblik**, thank you for sharing with me your remarkable story of courage, commitment and vision that is a key point of this book. I hope that I have conveyed your triumph in a way that will inspire my readers, just as you inspire me.

Frank Felsburg got behind *"The Six P's of Change"* early and pointed me to key resources, most notably, introducing me to Karen. Frank, I'm pleased that we have resumed the journey that started 25 years ago at The Charles Morris Price School. The teacher has indeed become a student.

To the memory of **Leonard K. Doviak**, who, during my years with him at General Electric Power Systems, taught me how to handle wrenching change — both professional and personal — with the utmost grace.

I am fortunate to have people in my life who, without lifting a pencil or editing a syllable, have kept me going simply because I know they are there: **Vince Burkett, Steve Fischer** and **Tobi Mackler, Barry** and **Mary Matus,** and **Bob** and **Amy Reif**. All I can say is thank you for every thoughtful little thing you have done for me over the last 40 years.

My mother and father, **Rita** and **Mario Rocchi,** helped support me as I made my way through life by knowing the difference between the things that I needed (e.g., an education, a typewriter) and the things I did not (e.g., sports equipment and power tools, both of which are very dangerous in my hands).

To my children, **Julia** and **Francis**, creative talents in their own right, who are now able to advise me on this book. (It's nice having smart, grown-up kids.) I know the day is coming when I will be much more famous for being their father than for anything I have done on my own. I'm looking forward to that.

Finally, last because she is first, my beautiful **Marie**. We dream together, we sing together, and you are one of my few constants among the changes I have endured in my life. I can write a book, speeches and more, but you still leave me grasping for words after 30 wonderful years.

This book is dedicated to my mother,
Rita Nancy Rocchi,
who not only gave me life,
but the sense of humor to handle it.

Same here, Mom!

TABLE OF CONTENTS

And now is the time to implement the Six P's of Change

> *"If you're in a bad situation, don't worry, it'll change. If you're in a good situation, don't worry, it'll change."*
> — John A. Simone, Sr.

INTRODUCTION

How much can sudden change affect you? Consider a lesson learned from a most unlikely event, the 1986 World Series, the championship of baseball.

The Boston Red Sox were playing the New York Mets in game six of the World Series. The Sox were perpetual also-rans, but they were up three games to two this year. With just one more win, they would earn their first championship in 68 years.

On this night, the Sox were playing the Mets in New York City. The Mets were also anxious to win, for they had not brought home a Series championship in 17 years, not since the "Miracle Mets" had won in 1969. After nine innings, the game was in a 3-3 tie. Boston took a 5-3 lead in the top of the tenth inning. In the bottom of the tenth, the Red Sox relievers struck out the Mets' first two batters. With only one more out, the Red Sox would win and break their long losing streak.

However, Gary Carter was the captain of the Mets and the team's spiritual leader that year. Carter hit a single to left field. A rally ensued, and soon the score was tied in the tenth inning. But, remember the Mets already had two outs. A simple out, just one more, would mean more innings and the Red Sox having another chance to win the game.

The Mets played Mookie Wilson. He hit a routine ground ball to veteran Red Sox first baseman Bill Buckner. The Boston fans were relieved. Buckner was sure to get the ball and tag first, leading to the eleventh inning and another chance at the game and the championship.

However, the usually reliable Buckner was playing on two bad ankles, and the unexpected happened. He dropped the ball. The final Mets runner came in, and the New Yorkers won the game, 6-5. Boston and New York played a seventh and deciding game. The Mets won that one, too, 8-5, beating the Red Sox for the world championship.

In the meantime, NBC was covering the collapse of the Red Sox World. The ratings for the series were just okay… until that last game. When the Red Sox and Mets played the seventh deciding game, the ratings were huge. More than half of all the TVs in use that night were tuned to baseball. Nearly five times as many viewers watched that game than were watching Monday Night Football, the perennial leader for Mondays in the fall. This timeframe was often referred to as "sweeps," a time when viewership and consumer response were tallied and assigned. So NBC used their huge ratings to set their advertising rates for the next few months. Such huge viewership was a windfall for them.

So Bill Buckner, an otherwise exemplary player, saw his team lose a coveted World Series title because of his error. He didn't live down that mistake for years. On the other hand, NBC benefited greatly from that event, despite never having such a plan. Change simply happened to the network.

Such is the nature of sudden, unexpected change. It can bring you fortune as it did for NBC. Or, it can darken your life for years as it did for Buckner. This one game serves as just a small example of change that occurred in the 20th century.

Consider the shifts that have occurred in the world since 1900. People once lived primarily on farms until industrialization brought about the new concept of a job. For the first times in many peoples' lives, they traveled away from their homes to work for somebody else and receive money in exchange. That money created an entirely new standard of living, which begat increased consumption, which begat the need for increased manufacturing, which begat even more new jobs.

In the late 19th and early 20th centuries, horses were common on city streets. In fact, there were so many of them that their waste was everywhere, and, when they died, their abandoned carcasses were often left to rot, creating a public health hazard. In the 20th century, automobiles became the most common method of trans-portation, creating a different but equal threat to public health as emissions were linked to respiratory diseases. Over time, with our need for oil to power our mechanical vehicles, there was a major shift in the world's economies. More and more money began to flow to oil-producing countries.

In other advancements, modern research on antibiotics began in 1909 for the treatment of syphilis. Antibiotics advanced later in Britain with the discovery of penicillin by Alexander Fleming in 1928. But as these new drugs became more powerful and effective in killing previously deadly diseases, they also led to the evolution of bacterial strains, even more dangerous and virulent. In the same time, the world saw the massive rise of communication media, evolving from radio and television to cell phones and per-sonal computers. The proliferation of these gadgets created more information and disseminated it more widely. Yet paradoxically, fewer people were actually speaking to each other, as eyes and ears tuned to devices rather than people.

Is this too big a picture, too much to comprehend? Let's narrow the focus to just a previous generation or two. After our grandparents or parents lived through World War II, they began to live through an unprecedented economic expansion. As the United States' economic competitors were generally knocked out by the war, this country had virtual control of the world's markets to itself. As U.S. companies grew richer, they often shared the wealth with their employees in the form of lucrative benefits and healthy union contracts. (The union negotiators of one world-famous industrial company admitted to me that lush union settlements were common in those days because it helped avoid the strikes that would slow down the delivery of products.) Layoffs were also uncommon in those days. On the other hand, if a person lost a job other companies usually could use their help. After retirement, many companies gave their employees pensions that carried them and their spouses through their golden years. The new middle class standard of living that was created in the early part of the century spread.

Now fast forward to today's world. The healthcare plans of most companies require a co-pay from the employee — if there is healthcare at all. Pensions are unusual; if you are lucky, you get a 401k with some sort of match. Companies think little of cutting back benefits or laying off employees to save costs in an uncertain world. Uncertain? Did I mention that American companies have many more competitors today? And that these competitors outside the U.S. usually are not bound to union contracts or minimum wage, advantages leading to much lower operating costs. This makes it tougher for U.S. employers to compete, so they must cut staff and reduce budgets.

In the course of my career as a professional communications expert, I have served corporations, organizations and individuals who needed to communicate, and deal with, change. Though the changes I communicated were not so wide-ranging as I described above, my messages always seemed to follow the same format:

1. Here is the world to which you are accustomed.

2. Here is the new world.

3. Here is the way you and I will deal with those changes.

When you consider all the transitions I have seen over the decades of my working life, whether they include the highs and lows of the economy, the fall and rise and fall again of manufacturing, or societal and cultural evolutions, I certainly have had much to ponder. Yet with all of the turmoil I have witnessed, you might think that I have become jaded about stability in this world of ours. You'd be mistaken; ultimately, I am an optimist. For example, I love every New Year, not for the parties, food or drink; instead, I see every New Year's Day as a time for renewal and reflection. One thing I can count on each New Year to bring is change, and I always hope and pray that change will be positive. But, changes like those described above come in many forms, often heart-rending and difficult. They can be divisive between you and your loved ones. On the other hand, they can also offer new and unforeseen opportunities, and they can change your outlook.

Despite my optimistic nature, I often find myself looking over my shoulder, suspecting that I could face very new, very un-positive circumstances in my life. Simply put, I have come to expect the unexpected. And, such an expectation is not a bad thing. In fact, I heartily recommend it, as expecting and accepting help us become the beneficiary of change rather than the victim of it.

This book allows me to share many perspectives from my career as a "change agent." I cite my own life experiences and those of others. My approach to this subject is organized according to a set of principles I call *The Six P's of Change.*

Step 1 — Develop the **PERCEPTION** that change is a reality.

Nobody is immune from change. I was not, although I was born into an America so fortunate that we all began to think that trees could grow to the sky. But I learned to recognize that change is inevitable, a theme that has become my life philosophy. Once I recognized change's inevitability, I lived my life accordingly, not in a constant state of paranoia, but, rather, in a state of preparedness.

Step 2 — Gain the **PERSPECTIVE** that change is often neither all positive nor all negative.

I have come to believe that the "good old days" are usually replaced by a set of good *new* days. Change is not automatically all good or all bad. It often depends on what you make of it. Positive change is bound to bring you good fortune if you are prepared to let it do so. Negative change is more difficult, but even that may be a catalyst for renewal or advancement if you turn that change to your advantage.

Step 3 — Learn the art of **PROGNOSTICATION**, which is all about predicting the future the best you can before the future happens to you.

Through awareness, education, and an alert attitude, you can learn to foretell change to some extent. There are experts out there who provide you with all the information you need *IF* you take the time to listen. Did you ever notice that some things seemed obvious in retrospect? ("Oh, I should have known that you were planning a surprise party for me!") That's because we realize the signs were there all along. We can learn to read many of those signs earlier and be that much ahead of the game.

Step 4 — Practice **PROACTIVE PREPARATION** for **whatever you see is coming down the road.**

Once you have a sense of changes that may be coming down the road, it is important to assess your preparedness to face them, whatever those changes may be. This is where your imagination can fly. For example, if things start to look shaky in your workplace, picture yourself as your own corporation — (YOUR NAME), Incorporated — an organization with a mission, a market, and profit center. To determine how competitive this new corporation will be, you must assess yourself honestly and thoroughly. Looking internally, what are your strengths and weaknesses? Looking to the outer world, what opportunities and threats lie ahead? If, in a different scenario, you show signs of change in your health, it is time to see your physician, get the diagnosis if there is one, and then plan the steps that will get you in the best form possible.

Step 5 — Develop **PLANNING** — a step-by-step strategy **that will meet your defined goals.**

Once you have assessed your skills and the external factors that may affect your future, it is important to take your thoughts and create a plan of action. You will learn about plans that kept the rich and famous as rich and famous as they were *before* they faced their own life-altering changes. In fact, many of them took calculated steps to surmount the odds they faced, and they thrived in the face of adversity.

Step 6 — Implement **P E R F O R M A N C E** of your plan, executing all of its elements superbly.

Writing down a plan is one thing. Bringing it to fruition is another. You must get into the mental discipline that is necessary to execute your plan and make it a reality. Yes, William Arthur Ward, one of America's most quotable and notable inspirational writers, was correct when he said, "If you can imagine it, you can achieve it. If you can dream it, you can become it." Unfortunately, imagination and dreaming are not enough. Many people read Mr. Ward's quote and stop there, rather than following steps toward attainment. The most important of our tasks is execution. We will discuss this notion later in the book.

The end of every chapter contains *An Intermission for Your Transition* — exercises that help guide you through your own experiences. They are designed to help bring your deepest thoughts to the front of your brain, where you can deal with them more effectively. In doing so, you can begin to build a plan that can either help you deal with immediate change or create a longer-range plan that will prepare you for transitions down the road

Okay, let's go. It's time to start your engines and head toward your first P.

> *"We live in a moment of history where change is so speeded up that we begin to see the present only when it is already disappearing."*
> — R. D. Laing, *British psychoanalyst and philosopher*

Step 1 — PERCEPTION

Change is a reality. Get used to it and recognize it.

If you think anyone is immune from change, then just look at this young 21st century. Think of what we have already seen that seemed to threaten the stability of our lives. Y2K. 9/11. Imagine that you worked for Enron for years, invested your retirement money into the company stock, and then saw it all essentially disappear. Witness the global economic changes in the U.S. of 2008, which were a confluence of the fall of American investment banking, widespread mortgage defaults, and the collapse of Detroit's automakers, all which affected many retirement plans. This turnabout has been called the greatest shock to American financial systems since the Great Depression.

Now think of the smaller changes you went through personally. You learned to walk… to ride a bike… you had a first day at school… a first day of work… a first date with an important someone… You may take these events for granted now, but they were changes to your life.

I know change from not only my own life, but also from seeing it happen to others during my career. I was once hired by a company that had been the leading producer of gas and steam turbines in the world. They built the largest turbine-generator ever, along with the largest nuclear plant in Japan. Then suddenly, they began to lose their world leadership. During the energy crisis of the 1970s, orders for new gas and steam turbines fell precipitously. Power requirements decreased as U.S. industry became more service-oriented and less industrial. The extensive regulation of utilities caused the postponement of large capital investments, including turbines.

Competition had also changed. After World War II, the U.S. had the power generation market to itself as foreign competitors were rebuilding their countries. Eventually, our old leader company had more than a dozen competitors. With all of these competitors came worldwide overcapacity.

The head of this business and his direct reports knew they had to take drastic actions across five states in order to keep the company viable. They closed and even demolished buildings to cut both operating costs and tax obligations. (You don't pay taxes on a building you don't have!) They reduced the salaried workforce. Manufacturing operations were consolidated, which shuttered some facilities and put its workers out of jobs. Inventory was reduced, and other unnecessary assets were sold off.

This leader knew that his actions were troublesome for many of the workers and their communities. In an address to employees, the leader expressed his concern about the pain and suffering that was occurring. "It's not much fun watching your friends go out the door in layoffs. It's not much fun watching buildings be torn down. On the other hand, the only alternative we have is the death of the business."

The actions, which first seemed Draconian, worked. Base costs, such as taxes, salaries and the maintenance of assets, were reduced. Inventory costs were also reduced by half. The corporate parent of the business had lent them hundreds of millions of dollars to fix their operations, and that loan was repaid early. This same company survives today as a world leader in the design and development of turbine technology. And they are prepared for the future, having invested in other forms of power generation, such as wind-driven turbines and hydropower.

But let's back up. How did this company arrive at the brink of extinction? They did not recognize the changes happening around them because their established paradigm did not allow them to *perceive the reality of change:*

- They could command the highest prices for their products. And because they were essentially the only turbine producer in the world, they passed huge pay increases to both their salaried and union employees.

- They did not maintain leadership in technology because, at the time, doing so was not necessary.

- They built more manufacturing facilities than they needed.

Robert Frost once said, "Most of the change we think we see in life is due to truths being in and out of favor." How true. Like the folks in this turbine business, we are often deluded into thinking that the world in which we operate behaves only in a certain way. When that way changes, we can suffer cognitive dissonance — a state of psychological conflict that comes from a contradiction with a person's long-held beliefs or attitudes. Think of the ways in which conflicts with change manifest themselves into statements of denial:

- "My children will have a higher standard of living than I do. Every new generation benefits from that." *Actually, in real terms, spending power has been decreasing for years in the U.S.*

- "My house will never go down in value. Real estate is the best investment there is." *The economic crisis of 2008 was the very result of an unforeseen downturn in home prices.*

- "The U.S. will always be the number one automaker in the world because our cars are better than the tin cans made in other countries." *We don't talk about the "Big Three" in the car world anymore; instead, it's the "Detroit Three," in recognition of how Toyota's sales first surpassed those of General Motors in 2007.*

Recognizing and adapting to change has little to do with willpower or intellect. One of the main determinants of success in life is the *readiness* for change. This is the ability to suspend our cognitive dissonance, our willingness to abandon entrenched beliefs and to *see the world as it really is, not the way we wish to see it.*

The leader of our troubled turbine business addressed this tendency when he charted the course to revitalization. He noted that many turbine industry analysts said that the future was hopeful on the surface. These analysts were forecasting continued growth based on an historical increase in electrical consumption. However, he disputed those forecasts, warning of the danger in blindly following such optimistic projections. He said that basing the future on historical assumptions was like "driving down the road at 50 mph while looking in the rear view mirror. Then you put the car in cruise control, jump in the back seat, and next thing you know, the car is in a ditch." He noted that many businesses were run according to predictable historical patterns.

So to be able to adjust to change when it comes your way, you must first perceive and recognize the reality that change is inevitable. And to help you handle change when it comes, remember this mantra: You can't control change; you can control only your reaction to it.

I got a double whammy of change in my next corporate assignment — change that first floored me and then prepared me mentally for the future.

When I was successful in my job as a communication manager in the turbine business, I became well known as a change agent in my company. I was offered a nice promotion to transfer to the division headquarters of one of our defense companies. The looming challenge? Some observers in the late 1980s had an inkling that the military-industrial market was about to change. That was not necessarily the conventional wisdom, because this period was just after President Ronald Reagan's administration ended. He had practiced a policy of "peace through strength," which resulted in a record peacetime defense buildup that included a 40 percent real increase in defense spending between 1981 and 1985.

However, that was to change. After President Reagan left office, defense spending became unpopular. For one thing, international tensions had decreased. Soviet Premier Mikhail Gorbachev stunned the world by announcing that he would cut a half-million solders from his country's European forces. This surprise proposal was viewed by many as an impetus to both U.S. and NATO defense cuts.

Liking the prospect of peace, the American public said they wanted to reduce the Department of Defense budget as a way to lower the overall budget deficit, according to a Gallup Poll of the time. After 1985, the real growth in defense appropriations started to decline. The new U.S. President, George Herbert Walker Bush, had nominated John Tower as Secretary of Defense. Even Tower, well known as a hawk on defense, began talking about sufficient defense at lower costs. Defense contracts were "stretched out," meaning that the Pentagon saved money by delaying the start of production runs.

And like our turbine business, the defense industry experienced challenges from an unlikely source: foreign competition. U.S. defense contractors were no more immune to a changing world than the auto industry. Indeed, their share of the international defense market started to erode, dropping from 36 percent to the low 30s in five years. A study by the Defense Science Board had concluded that as these countries became more sophisticated, they teamed up to beat the U.S. at its own game.

So the U.S. defense industry's boom years ended. There was a grim joke among defense contractors after President Reagan left office that went something like this: "Our market retired and went back to California!" However, unlike those in the turbine industry, the leaders of the defense industry, as well as its analysts, saw this change coming. Because of that I was able to put together a program that prepared all interested parties — including employees, elected officials, the local media, and the community — for this upcoming change that would affect so many in this mid-sized town in upstate New York. I helped give these stakeholders tools to handle their lives beyond the change.

I compiled, wrote and published studies that made readers aware of the evolution in defense. I encouraged managers and supervisors to hold meetings with their employees to discuss these issues. (I published notes to which they could refer during their employee meetings so that our managers were literally "all on the same page.") I met with local elected leaders to prepare them so that they were not embarrassed. Finally, I built up my relationship with the local media. They knew to come to me with any rumors they picked up so we could discuss and clarify them. I also trusted that my company's side of the story would be told fairly when a big announcement came. And, that announcement wasn't long in coming.

On a Friday morning in the spring, I delivered the dreaded news. We were cutting 800 jobs, which would have a huge impact in a town of 55,000. The Saturday edition of the local paper had a banner headline about the layoffs. But there was also a subhead that read, "People worried, but think the company cares." Echoing that sentiment, a 37-year employee was pictured on the front page with a quote: "I have faith in the company."

So while this event was certainly not bloodless, neither was it a catastrophe. People were mentally prepared because they had learned that downsizing was a real possibility. We had worked with the state and other civic organizations to put training programs in place for the affected employees. Over the next few months, people were trained for new positions and many of them found work. There were similar efforts that I coordinated in the other locations in our division; they were also well executed. Overall, my efforts were deemed a success.

Yet I could not help but feel that there were more changes coming … changes that were bound to affect me. The first indication was an announcement that the division headquarters would change location. We got a new vice president to lead the division, and he moved the headquarters closer to his home. This meant that I was not geographically close to him or the other business leaders anymore. If I wanted to meet with them, I had to drive 90 minutes, which was not very convenient, especially in the snowy upstate New York weather. More damaging, I did not have their ears. Those of us from that "other location" were seen as intruders and interlopers. When the headquarters changed, so did the center of gravity for the division. My influence began to diminish, but I figured my job was safe. I had just come off a huge success with the announcement and my overall leadership, so there was no reason to remove me, right?

Wrong. In less than a year after the layoff announcement, consolidations in the business were announced. The new company leadership decided to have a manager in another location lead the communication for the business.

I couldn't believe it! I argued in my own head. *"I had built the communications organization from practically nothing. I had won the corporation's highest communication award while I was in that job. Twice! I was married with two small children. I had relocated for the company. After all that I did for them, how could they do this?"* I asked the question so many people ask at such times. *"Why me?"*

Eventually, I answered the question myself. "Why NOT me?"

What made me think that I was special? Was I in a privileged class? The business still needed to be competitive. They needed to consolidate. Yes, what was happening to me was not easy or pleasant, but I had to deal with it.

I learned about my job elimination on a Friday, and when I learned the details of my benefits package, they ameliorated my concerns. First, I would be on salary for another six months, which I found to be more than fair; it was downright generous. I also received outplacement services, which meant that I would get help in searching for a job. The only problem was there were no offices of the outplacement agency in this small town. I commuted weekly to my home town of Philadelphia. There I learned or re-learned many of the skills I would need to not only find a new job but also manage my career in the future.

One day in the outplacement office, one of the other clients told me that she had been released as director of public relations and communications from one of the Philadelphia's most historic hospitals, one with an international reputation for excellence in pediatrics. The job was still open, and I was confident that I had the communications credentials for the position. I had also worked for a healthcare-related company once, so I reasoned that I could work for a hospital. So I contacted the hospital and applied for the position. After reviewing my application, they promptly informed me in a letter that they would not consider me for the job at that time. They wished me luck in my endeavors.

I responded as only a true professional would. I called the manager of employment and told her they were making a big mistake!

I had done my homework, and I argued that they needed me because healthcare was undergoing a great deal of change. I knew that reimbursements were diminishing, mostly due to the rise of health maintenance organizations. Also, hospitals were consolidating in order to save costs. What other candidate had as much experience in communicating change to a wide variety of stakeholders, such as the caregivers (physicians and nurses), patients and their families, employees, local elected leaders, and the community? I had precisely the skills they needed. Or at least that's what I told them.

Somewhat reluctantly, they added me to the list of candidates, the tenth of 10. (I suspect this was at least partially due to their desire to get me off their backs.) I made it through the interviews and, to the chagrin of local healthcare communicators who were more experienced, I got the job.

My corporate experience served me well within my first year when the hospital's workers decided to strike. Strikes are unusual in hospitals, so many healthcare communicators don't have the experience in dealing with them. But I did have experience of communicating management's side of strike issues. Within a week of the start of the strike, the union signed a contract — the contract that was on the table when the strike started! My communication with the local media led to favorable press, and the union was unable to curry favorable public opinion. Soon the body of healthcare communicators in the Philadelphia region invited me to their meetings to discuss my strategies and analyze why they worked. I had not only returned to my hometown; I had also arrived as a proven expert in an entirely new field.

This entire experience — ranging from communicating change in the defense industry, finding myself out of work, and then remaking myself to revitalize my career — brought home to me the lessons I had tried to teach my stakeholders in the corporate world: change is inevitable, and it is unavoidable. Yet I learned firsthand that by changing the interior of my attitudes, my prejudices and my mind, I could change the external features of my life. This has become my philosophy — not an obsession, but a recognition. I do my best to live my life accordingly, not in a constant state of paranoia, but in a state of preparedness.

Lessons from Step 1

1. Change around us is inevitable.

2. The change we make is often the only alternative to extinction.

3. When faced with change, we often suffer cognitive dissonance — a state of psychological conflict that comes from a contradiction with a person's long-held beliefs or attitudes. We must learn to overcome that condition and see the world as it really is, not the way we wish to see it.

4. It is dangerous to base personal or business decisions solely on historical precedence and assumptions. Our paradigms can change.

5. You cannot control change. You can control only your reaction to it.

6. You can change your situations by applying your existing knowledge and talents to new opportunities.

7. To handle change capably, it is best to live a life of preparedness, not one of paranoia.

Intermission For Your Transition

Let's Review the Ranges of your Personal Changes.

Review the following questions and jot down your *IMMEDIATE* answers. Write *AS MANY* as come to your mind, even if you need extra sheets of paper.

1. **Write a list of changes you have experienced in your life that you initiated yourself and made happen.** *(Examples: choosing a spouse or other life partner; pursuing an academic degree or trade.)*

_____

_____

_____

_____

_____

_____

_____

2. **Write a list of changes you have experienced in your life that were imposed on you.** *(Examples: a life-changing accident, an unexpected job loss or decline in your business.)*

_____

_____

_____

_____

_____

_____

_____

3. **Compare the answers in 1 and 2. How did these events change your life in the *short* term?**

_____

_____

_____

_____

_____

_____

_____

4. How did they change your life over the *long* term?

_____

_____

_____

_____

_____

_____

_____

Think about these. Keep them in mind as we head to the next P of Change.

> *"Turbulence is life force. It is opportunity.*
> *Let's love turbulence and use it for change."*
> — Former U.S. Attorney General Ramsay Clark

Step 2 — PERSPECTIVE

Change is usually neither all positive nor all negative.

I have come to embrace change in my life once I accepted the concept that, while it is inevitable, it is not necessarily threatening. Prior to the start of the 20th century, change was not so obvious. In fact, most people did not lead hopeful lives. The life they were born into was likely to be the one they would lead, as so much was determined by factors outside of their control, such as family wealth, race or gender. Where such change once occurred incrementally, it comes at us today at a dizzying pace. Sometimes it is life altering; occasionally it is life-ending. We can deal with it better when we develop our speed and agility. Doing so increases our ability to achieve better personal results in the face of change.

My wife and I were both fortunate to learn about the scope of change by observing our grandmothers, both of whom lived into their mid-90s. We were awed by what these two immigrants saw in their lifetimes as they lived the American century. They went from walking on dirt streets in Italy to speeding across the U.S. on superhighways. In their old age, both flew in airplanes, which were not even invented when they were born. (Imagine the implications of that; what mode of transportation will we use in the future that doesn't currently exist?) Diseases like polio and measles, which once threatened their children with disability or even death, were virtually wiped out. They read about a worldwide war, the first ever, in newspapers. When they sent their sons to serve in a second one, they received updates and pep talks through that piece of furniture in their parlors, the radio. Over time, they would come to see their grandsons' war in Asia. Viet Nam came to be called the "living room war," because it became a regular part of the evening's television programming.

In their younger days, they would have received the news of a president's death in a day or two. In their later years, they heard that President Kennedy was shot within an hour of the event, and two days later, they saw his accused assassin killed on live television.

Consider now the opportunities provided to our grandmothers' descendants by the change they witnessed. Change creates ripples through our economy as the pulling of a single thread may alter the fabric of an entire garment. The automobile age created the need for professional mechanics, and it drove many saddle-makers out of business. The protection of drivers, passengers, and pedestrians created the auto insurance industry, and financial institutions like the General Motors Acceptance Corporation were created to allow consumers to buy autos.

The growth of cities gave birth to urban planning, which sometimes wiped out whole neighborhoods to make way for roads. The airplanes that did not exist prior to our grandmothers' births eventually became so numerous that society needed air traffic controllers. And so it has been with other technological and cultural developments. Television brought entertainment and global communication into our homes, but it also contributed to decreased reading, less time for families to speak with each other, and that nutritional milestone, the TV dinner. Computers once took up an entire floor of a company's building. Today, there is one in every office or cubicle, an indispensable link to informative databases and co-workers an ocean away. However, it has also spawned a new set of orthopedic problems as workers are tied to their desks. The iPod® not only revolutionized the way we hear (and see) our entertainment, but other industries are making room for it, such as in their auto sound systems or their denim jeans.

So I recognize that change is not always welcome. It definitely comes with a yin and a yang. Let me be clear that I do not idealize it, romanticize it, or minimize it. While changes often come with unique benefits, there may also be considerable downsides. Industry and large-scale manufacturing have brought goods to the world, as well as other wealth in the form of gainful employment, offering alternatives to our agrarian societies. However, unfettered expansion of the industrial world has also brought pollution to air, land and water. Similarly, the decline of our cities is a change, and we have not welcomed that or other deterioration.

I believe that people often reveal their characters by their reactions to the circumstances presented to them. One example comes from Thomas Edison, one of the greatest Americans of all time, certainly of the 20th century. He held nearly 1,100 patents that ranged from the incandescent lamp and motion pictures to a device for breaking up rocks. Yet despite his accomplishments and good fortune, Edison experienced a setback that would have devastated most other men. Fortunately, Edison was not like most other men.

In 1914, Edison's famous laboratory in West Orange, New Jersey, was destroyed by fire. Edison watched as much of his life's work literally went up in smoke. He was advanced in years at this point – age 67, well past the life expectancy of his era – so, to him, this might have seemed the end of his legacy. But he approached the situation with the stoic optimism that marked his entire life. According to Robert Conot's biography of Edison, *"A Streak of Luck"*:

"Someone brought Edison a photograph of himself that, although it had been in one of the destroyed buildings, had escaped unscathed. 'Never touched me,' he [Edison] scrawled across it… One week after the fire, the debris was gone. [A few weeks later], the Phonograph works went back into production."

Edison faced potentially terrifying change that fiery night. He did not let it deter him from living up to his life's mission. In fact, he approached it with his typical sense of awe and wonderment – the qualities that made him so successful as an inventor in the first place. He lived up to his own motto, "Have faith and go forward."

Edison's trials also give evidence to another truth that we often overlook in our vanities: We will not be shielded from change by our youth or our age, our wealth, our education, or our fame. None of us is entitled to a life of comfortable consistency, unburdened by adjustments. Because of that fact, we can take satisfaction in our triumphs over change. They can be life-affirming events that embolden us for future challenges. In fact, many people fear failure much less once they have overcome the consequences of misfortune. Unfortunately, many of us allow our failures to keep us from even trying to develop new abilities or take a risk. Indeed, we often do not see our full range of capabilities because we protect ourselves from the challenging circumstances that would bring them out. We certainly did not have those inhibitions as children. We probably would not have learned to walk, talk, or use a toilet if we allowed ourselves to be intimidated by the times we fell, mumbled, or soiled our underwear. Yet as adults, we let the fear of failure keep us from learning a new language, using a new tool like a computer or camera, or dancing. Like ignorance, the fear of failure is very expensive.

In my role as an agent of change, I did not experience only negative situations in business. There was more to see than business downturns and layoffs; I have seen positive change, too, but even that can be challenging. This was the case when my company transferred me to a defense business in Daytona Beach, Florida that made flight simulators. Based on my previous experiences that I cited in this book, you may have already inferred that the organization needed me because they were undergoing a business contraction and cancelled contracts. Actually, it was quite the opposite. Business was booming. The year before I arrived, they made eleven flight simulators. In my first year on the job, they made 88 — an eightfold increase without a commensurate increase in employees.

And therein was the challenge. Employee output was *growing*. People were working more than ever... and they saw that as a problem! They felt their tools were not up-to-date. Materials ran out at times. And the quickened pace created tensions among people who were used to leisurely workdays. Many people in the Rust Belt at that time would have *loved* to have such problems. Still, this was the situation, and I was transferred there to help change the tone.

I started an employee communication program that emphasized how well business was going. I highlighted the new contracts. I profiled the accomplishments of employees throughout the organization, emphasizing the contributions from the factory floor rather than those from the executive suite. Yet there was still something nagging the folks there. When we had employee lunches with the local president, they often turned into confrontational, even angry sessions about the materials, the tools, and so on.

We had our opportunity to turn things around at the annual employee meeting. This event was a favorite tradition, which was established long before I had arrived. The business would rent out the jai alai court next door, create a large screen video production, and have members of management present on their own parts of the company. The employees enjoyed this meeting because it was their one day a year to learn about the state of the business and the plans for the future. However, in that year we tried a different approach. To plan the meeting, we interviewed long-term employees about what they thought of the present business compared to years before.

The interviews revealed that long-term employees were very happy with their *existing* stability when they compared it to the recent past. At one time, the business was so tenuous that there were layoffs every week. They remembered "Pink Slip Fridays" — the layoffs that happened regularly at the end of each work week.

We determined that overtime, material shortages, the hustle and bustle of the plant were all *good* things, because they showed that the business was healthy. As a result of this insight, we designed our big screen presentation to feature a fictional vendor who serviced our soda machines. He shared his "view" of the business over the past 20 years as an impartial observer who had seen people come and go, yet he had never seen the business as healthy as it was at that moment. Furthermore, he told his story through a song called "Growin' Pains," which was written in the style of country music, definitely a plus with that particular audience, adding a light-hearted tone to the message. The employee audience was snapping their fingers and singing along, but they were also getting the message through lyrics like these:

> *Well, I guess what we're going through is growin' pains.*
>
> *And I guess right at first it might seem mighty strange.*
>
> *But since we're working hard, it shows we've come so far;*
>
> *I'll take this over "Pink Slip Friday" any day of the week!*

All of a sudden, having lots of work did not seem so bad. And the lesson came through clearly: you can't control change, but you can control how you react to it. And you can't assume the change is negative; in this case, it was very positive. With a change in perspective, people stopped complaining. Instead, they learned to appreciate the opportunities they had received.

The reality is that we cannot live in the past. We will reside only in the future, so we should prepare for it as we do any destination and welcome it as a place to thrive. Times of change underline the importance of leadership, both organizational and personal. Cardinal John Henry Newman, a great leader of the Catholic Church in America, said, "Let us take things as we find them; let us not attempt to distort them into what they are not. We cannot make facts. All the wishing in the world cannot change them. We must use them."

My children and other younger people I know, rarely, if ever, hear me use the phrase, "Back in the good old days..." I believe that as time advances, the "good old days" are usually replaced by a set of good new days. Change is not necessarily binary; it's not automatically all good or all bad. History records many positive results from what may seem like the worst possible circumstances. For example, the Second World War, though terrible, helped lift the American standard of living for several generations. When soldiers returned home, there was pent-up demand for all kinds of goods, such as cars, homes, and appliances. There seemed to be no end to the demand. And many European suppliers were out of commission because they were destroyed by the war. So there were many opportunities for Americans who were ready. All this led to the greatest expansion of the middle class in our nation's history.

If you are reading this book as a company leader, then you should think of your responsibilities in influencing the people around you to anticipate and handle change. If your scope of interest is your own personal life, then you should exercise the same leadership for your loved ones, whether acting as a parent, spouse, or other family member. Notice that I said *leadership*, not *authority*. An effective leader frames change so that others can first understand it and then come to grips with it. Authority alone cannot force others to deal with change effectively. Reverend Theodore Hesburgh, who served as Notre Dame's President for 35 years, said, "The very essence of leadership is that you have to have a vision."

I would add that if vision doesn't allow you to see the fog of change ahead of time, it will at least show you the way to navigate through it. John W. Gardner, a social philosopher who founded Common Cause and author of the book *"Self-Renewal,"* advocated the development of the following habits that will be useful in new situations:

- **Curiosity**

- **Open-mindedness**

- **Objectivity**

- **Respect for evidence**

- **The capacity to think critically**

All of these qualities reveal an energetic and facile mind that will be prepared for change. Curiosity is at the very heart of intellectual and personal growth. Think of the people you encounter at work and through friends and family. Curious people develop new hobbies, read new books, meet new people, and as a result, they continually expand their views, just as one does when ascending a mountain.

Think of the dullest people you know, and I will bet that you will find they are also among the least curious. I would guess that they stopped finding new things to learn, do, or know. As a result, they have no great stories to tell about their lives because they haven't done anything new in years. They probably use terms that became outmoded 15 years ago. They are typically stuck in an era, as a Model T could be stuck in the mud with no way out, ultimately becoming a symbol of a bygone time.

One person who continually amazed me with his vigorous intellect was the comedian George Carlin. He made people laugh for more than 50 years, and he was successful because he was always made sure to be relevant. One of his bits that I heard in the weeks before he died contained a litany of current terms, and he asserted that he would not fall victim to them. He would not be "downloaded" or "outsourced!" But he was on "beta blockers," and he was most decidedly an "alpha male." He always had the curiosity to be engaged in society *as it was at that moment*, not as he merely remembered it.

The close-minded, on the other hand, take in little or no information, as they choose not to have their provincial views challenged. Instead, they rely on their punchlines and slogans about the world, as they have long given up on real inspection of topics and issues. In their views, the world is neatly and conveniently divided into two camps:

1. The usual suspects who are responsible for all of society's ills (e.g., the media, military spending), and

2. The heroes who share their space on the political spectrum and can do no wrong.

In their minds, crimes are committed by the same types of people, government doesn't spend money on their priorities, and *their* political party has all the answers, regardless of the skills, intellect, and abilities of the candidates.

An open-minded, expansive attitude is also important to life at home and on the job. An introspective person may consider the following:

- What are the skills I need to function better in my job or even advance in my organization? Am I current on my technological tools? Do I provide value?

- What might be the future of my company or business? How well does it compete in the current economy?

- What are my transferrable skills if my current employment ended tomorrow? In fact, have I even considered that my job could end, or do I believe I have a "job for life?"

- How is my health? When was my last check-up? Could I be surprised if I had a complete blood test? Have I had symptoms that I have ignored?

- How do I maintain my health? Do I exercise enough? Do I have habits that could cause negative effects over time, such as drinking, smoking, or a poor diet?

- How is my relationship with my family? Am I aware of their concerns? Do I know where and how they spend their time?

- Have I planned for my future and the future of those closest to me?

We don't suffer the consequences of our actions alone; sometimes our *inaction* has a cost in missed opportunity or neglect of an important aspect of our lives. Those who accept change as a reality tend to have an open mind about all the possibilities in their lives and can prepare for them.

Time magazine chose Albert Einstein as the Person of the 20th Century. This quote provides some insight into the source of his great influence: "One cannot help but be in awe when he contemplates the mysteries of eternity, of life, of the marvelous structure of reality. It is enough if one tries merely to comprehend a little of this mystery every day. Never lose a holy curiosity."

So what does it take to succeed in a changing world? Absent the factor of luck (good or bad), it takes awareness of the very existence of change, openness to the various ways it can affect us, and ongoing self-analysis and renewal to deal with it. Consider these people who faced seemingly insurmountable odds and went on to achieve great things:

• A young boy named Louis was playing with tools in his father's harness shop when an awl slipped and pierced his eye. Ophthalmia set in, and the boy became blind. Despite this handicap, he became an excellent organist and cellist. At age 10, he received a scholarship to attend the National Institute for Blind Children in Paris, and by age 17, he began teaching there. During his time as a student, Louis was interested in developing a system of writing for the blind. At age 15, he adapted an established system of dots embossed on cardboard, and by age 20, he published a dissertation on his system.

Today, more than 175 years later, Louis Braille's system of printing and writing for the blind is accepted around the world. Ironically, he developed it using the very instrument that took his sight, the awl.

• John Wilson was born in Manchester, England, in 1917. He studied English language and literature at Manchester University. He wrote his first novel, "*A Vision of Battlement*," under his two middle names, Anthony Burgess, in 1949. However, the novel was not published for six years. In the interim, Burgess became an education officer in Malaya and Brunei, where he wrote three novels set in Malaya, which has come to be known as his Malayan Trilogy (1956-1959). In 1960, he was diagnosed with a cerebral tumor and given twelve months to live. In order to provide for his wife, he took up writing full time. The diagnosis turned out to be wrong, and he lived another 33 years. In that time, he was quite prolific, producing novels, articles, biographies, critical studies, even musical compositions. Burgess's best-known work was *"A Clockwork Orange,"* his 1962 dystopian novel that famed director Stanley Kubrick turned into a major film. Burgess died in 1993. What would his legacy have been if he had not been spurred to action by a misdiagnosis of imminent death?

- Jo, a single welfare mother in the U.K. was on a train trip from Manchester to London in 1990 when she thought of a children's story that she would like to write. Because of prejudice against women, she thought it would be better to use just the initials of her first and middle names. In just a few years, J. K. Rowling became world-famous as the author of the Harry Potter fantasy series. She is equally famous for her Horatio Alger-like biography, rising from poverty to multi-millionaire status in just a few years. In 2008, *The Sunday Times* Rich List estimated Rowling's fortune at $1.1 billion, which made her the 12th richest woman in Britain. In a commencement address that same year, she told graduates, "You might never fail on the scale I did, but some failure in life is inevitable. It is impossible to live without failing at something, unless you live so cautiously that you might as well not have lived at all - in which case, you fail by default." Rowling chose not to be cautious and today she is credited with raising reading to a new level among school age children around the world.

LESSONS FROM STEP 2

1. Change may seem threatening, but it may also create opportunities.

2. More than ever, our lives may be governed by changes we choose.

3. Leadership is key in framing change and putting it in its proper perspective.

4. One cannot force others to deal with change. To handle change, we must embrace it willingly.

5. Developing vision is key to handling change, whether leading others or managing our own circumstances.

6. We must be open to all information and all points of view to understand fully the changes we are facing.

7. One cannot succeed in the face of change without risking failure.

Intermission For Your Transition

We Know Change is Inevitable. How Then Can We React to It?

Go back to the list you created of changes in your life and review your recollections of how those changes affected you. Use that information to review the following questions. Again, jot down your *IMMEDIATE* answers, and write *AS MANY* as you have.

1. **Knowing what you know today, how would you react to those changes in your life?** *(Examples: more time off from work after a job loss, retreat from the social scene after the end of a personal relationship.)*

_____

_____

_____

_____

_____

_____

2. **When reflecting on your life changes, how did they turn out differently than you first thought?** *(Examples: college did not fulfill your needs as your parents told you it would, or that new love in your life was not all you believed s/he would be.)*

_____

_____

_____

_____

_____

_____

_____

3. **List organizations that expose you to other people, preferably those whose viewpoints are different from yours.** *(Examples: a bowling league dominated by members of a distinct ethnic background, a book club with a wide variety of social and cultural viewpoints.)*

_____

_____

_____

_____

_____

_____

_____

4. List other ways you are exposed to new or challenging ideas.
_(Examples may range from publications with a different political
perspective to your first course in computers, which you may have
presumed you would never understand, to joining the local Toastmasters when you were terrified of speaking.)_

_____

_____

_____

_____

_____

_____

5. Write down risks you have taken in your life. How did they turn out?

_____

_____

_____

_____

_____

_____

_____

How easily could you answer these questions? Are you truly open to many new viewpoints or learning new skills? How deep are your lists? If they are long and varied, then congratulations, you have done more to keep your mind fresh than you realized. If the lists are shallow, perhaps you have not been as open-minded as you would like to think.

The ability to seek out and process information is important as we go to the next P of Change, which is all about foresight.

> *"Coming events cast their shadows before."*
> — Thomas Campbell,
> *19th century English attorney and poet*

Step 3 — PROGNOSTICATION

Predict the future in order to effect change rather than merely being affected by it.

Predicting the future to create a new paradigm may sound difficult, and it can be. However, it is possible. Once you accept that change is inevitable, you can learn to predict it with reasonable accuracy. No, you don't need to pay a fortuneteller; you only need to pay attention. Here are some examples of correct predictions that yielded big results:

- Steve Jobs could see that the public was ready to have their own computers as another home appliance. In 1977, his company introduced the Apple II and began the era of the personal computer. Today, PCs are a household's third biggest investment after their homes and their cars. (A prolific predictor, Jobs later saw that the public wanted to carry music with them easily, so Apple developed the iPod.)

- Mr. King Gillette — yes, his first name was King — was shaving one day when he imagined that men might want to do away with their straight razors. He imagined that they would like to use a blade and then just throw it away. His idea took hold when he distributed razors and blades to U.S. soldiers during World War I. This group formed the start of Gillette's loyal customer base, kicking off the use of many disposable items today.

- New York Governor DeWitt Clinton predicted that a canal con-
necting the Hudson River with the Great Lakes could improve
the economy of his state. He was thought to be mad, for the
project would cost an amount equal to one percent of the entire
country's gross domestic product (an amount roughly equivalent
today to more than $110 billion). The endeavor — which came
to be the Erie Canal — would also require moving a volume of
earth and rock equivalent to more than three times the volume
of the Great Pyramid in Egypt. When the federal government
declined to help, he managed to build the canal entirely through
state funds. His foresight resulted in a series of fortunes that
eventually led to the establishment of New York as the financial
capital of the world. It also ushered in the American belief that
we could complete big projects whether it was building the
Brooklyn Bridge, digging the Panama Canal, or putting a man
on the moon.

As shown in these examples, successful prediction can result from
research, observation, good old gut instinct, or a combination of
these. Some people don't believe in predictions, just as some don't
believe in alien abductions or chiropractors. Predictions have a bad
reputation. It's very popular to cite George Bernard Shaw's famous
observation that "If all economists were laid end to end, they
would not reach a conclusion." But, you don't often hear Shaw's
opposing quote: "The power of accurate observation is commonly
called cynicism by those who have not got it."

I propose that history shows that expert knowledge in a particular
subject, mixed with a familiarity with cause and effect over time,
often leads one to foresee future trends. The key to successful
prognostication is research — disciplined painstaking research. There
is a wide variety of available information for the insight you seek,
which may come from experts, seminars and journals. However,

you must take the time to find them and use them. Prediction starts with a notion of what you are trying to know. The next step is uncovering the information that will either support or refute your hypothesis. Finding out takes time, patience and, most importantly, an open mind. Sometimes, due to our human nature, we go through the motions of gathering information while closed to information that may refute our opening premises. But if we retain a sense of wonder and curiosity, research can be adventurous because we cannot always know where it will lead us.

H. G. Wells (1866 – 1946) is the model of a future-oriented thinker. Though best remembered today as a science fiction writer, he was also an observer of scientific phenomena. He used his knowledge and logic to predict a number of trends and developments over the course of the 20th century. Considered to have an overall accuracy rate of 60 to 80 percent, his predictions covered a wide range of subjects, such as urban living, transportation, government, defense methods, education and sociology. In a 1902 address to the Royal Society of England, he gave insight into his methodologies:

- **INDUCTIVE REASONING** — Wells taught that inductive reasoning — the process of making inferences by observed repetitive patterns — was key to making reasonably accurate predictions.

- **FUTURE-FOCUSED THINKING** — Wells did not live in the past. Instead, he thought constantly of things to come, and he believed that change could not be ignored. He also thought of the present in terms of how it could drive the future. This was an extension to the notion that the conditions of the past would drive the future.

- **GROUNDING IN SCIENCE** — Wells kept himself knowledgeable of scientific principles and developments, as he believed that science was predictive by nature. For example, he flew in the face of the thinking of his time by predicting that aircraft would be heavier than air, rather than lighter than air, as with balloons and dirigibles. His reasoning was that if a craft were to conquer the air, it would need to be stronger than air.

• **KNOWLEDGE OF THE PAST** — Wells believed that all future events were preordained by past events, so it was important to know the past in order to know the future.

• **LAW OF LARGE NUMBERS** — Wells used statistical probability to make predictions. He believed that while small, incremental human events may influence outcomes in some way, broad trends can tell the story more accurately, smoothing out the effects of anomalous events. Another way of saying this is that Wells looked at the big picture.

Wells used the following process to make his predictions:

1. Assume that prediction is possible.

2. Use a combination of facts, logic and math.

3. Gather data.

4. Identify the drivers in science and technology that could change the future.

5. Identify central tendencies using the science of statistics.

6. Identify the areas that will affected by change.

7. Pursue causal changes.

How accurate was Wells? In 1901, his book, *Anticipations*, predicted what the world would be like in the year 2000. He wrote that trains and cars would move workers between the cities and the suburbs, that women would seek and achieve greater sexual freedom, that there would be two world wars in which German militarism would be defeated, and that a European Union would be formed.

Ways to get information

H.G. Wells was among the first of a group of people called "futurists," whose occupation or specialty is the forecasting of future events, conditions, or developments. Even they don't get everything absolutely, positively correct every single time, but they are considered successful if they're accurate 60 percent of the time. (That's a pretty tough standard. Compare it to a baseball player who needs only to connect with a ball three out of ten times at bat to be called a "good hitter.")

Many business leaders use future studies as a way to plan properly. As H. G. Wells showed, the skill of **trend assessment** — the ability to identify and decipher trends — is important to success in future studies. Organizations that use future-oriented thinking are often able to achieve a significant edge in their markets. World trends and forecasts are based on a variety of factors including demographics, economics, environmental resources and habitats, government affairs (both in the U.S. and around the world), and science and technology. Think of some of these factors and how they may influence our lives and professions:

- **Demographics** — As the baby boomer population begins to decline in numbers, how will that affect the sales of products associated with that group? Will the decline of CD sales and the associated increase in musical downloads continue? Will jeans be replaced by another type of trousers, simply based on preference of the succeeding generation?

- **Economics** — Will home ownership decline as mortgages become more expensive or even more difficult to obtain?

- **Environment** — How will global warming, whether real or imagined and regardless of the cause, affect populations? Will people come to avoid locales that are feared to be "too hot?" Will real estate values in those areas drop?

- **Government affairs** — How do a country's restrictions on immigration affect their labor costs? Is it possible that limiting immigration leads to fewer workers and therefore increases labor rates?

- **Science and technology** — How does the ability to transfer word documents over the Internet affect the use of fax machines? May faxes even cease to exist? If you work as a technician on fax machines, is your future employment in jeopardy?

It is also important to understand the false signals that can lead you in a wrong direction and toward a wrong conclusion. For example, for the many people who thought that housing values would increase forever, they were rudely disappointed by the housing crisis of 2008. An earlier example was the faulty research that led Coca-Cola to believe that they needed to have a drink that tasted more like Pepsi. This belief led to New Coke, an historic marketing disaster. Apple and Nike are sterling examples of the ability to identify and capitalize on future trends. The American car industry is not.

There is a preponderance of information available to us through many media. The most successful individuals and organizations tend to access that information. Doing so helps them make more informed decisions in an ever more competitive and complicated world. Some sources of information include:

- **THE INTERNET** — You can have news pushed to your email. Check your favorite search engine and see what is available to you. For example, I receive the latest news in the healthcare industry throughout the day because that is the bulk of my marketing activities.

- **PROFESSIONAL ORGANIZATIONS** — Do you work in information technology? Auto mechanics? Perhaps you are a professional philosopher. However, you make a living, there is an organization for you that can provide new methodologies in your workplace and inform you of overall trends in your industry.

- **MAGAZINES** — There are certainly many general interest magazines that can help keep you informed of a wide variety of issues and developments, such as *Time* or *Newsweek*. However, there are also many specialty magazines to help you stay abreast of trends in very specific fields of interest. Example fields may include cooking, collectibles, military matters, and veterinary medicine. (I particularly recommend that you go to your library and review *The Futurist* magazine. It is published bi-monthly by the World Future Society, and I have found it to be an unbiased clearinghouse of ideas. Contributors over the years have included Gene Roddenberry, Buckminster Fuller, Isaac Asimov, and many others. For example, I read about the African AIDS epidemic in *The Futurist* about six years before it became a worldwide cause.)

- **SEMINARS** — Would you like to learn how to build a deck at home? Would you like to start a blog? You should be able to find a means of learning anything that will enhance your personal or professional life. Such sessions may be available at the local community college, the local leading hardware store, or even at the Y, and you need not invest a whole semester to your subject of choosing. A few nights over a month or even a single weekend may be all you need.

- **BOOKS** — There are so many places to obtain books that there is nothing keeping you from building a personal library. In addition to bookstores and online booksellers, there are sales at your local library and sales in neighborhood garages. If you don't want to accumulate so many books, just borrow them.

Some stores offer book swaps so that you can keep a fresh supply of reading materials available. You can even purchase the old books from your library and then contribute them back when you are finished, allowing someone else to enjoy them.

• AUDIO-VISUAL MEDIA — If you don't have time in your schedule to read or attend seminars and meetings, you may be able to pick up information from a variety of audio-visual media. You can schedule time to listen to audio (e.g., CDs, tapes, downloads from the Web) in your car, in the house, or through a personal player, such as an iPod. You can also use DVDs and old-fashioned videotapes in the comfort of your home.

We have long lived in "The Information Age." We can all learn what we need to know from a variety of sources. Dig deep into your imagination to find them, and dig deep into yourself to determine your commitment to getting the information you need to meet the challenges of a changing world.

Beyond Research

Some predictions don't require massive research. Sometimes we can rely on a combination of instincts and logic rather than purely rational analysis to see ahead. As the great philosopher Yogi Berra once said, "You can see a lot just by observing." Often you can make a fast and accurate investigation by analyzing the evidence right in front of you. When this happens and we call it "intuition," it is really wisdom and insight born of our cumulative life experiences — a concept depicted in books like *Blink* by Malcolm Gladwell and *Sources of Power: How People Make Decisions* by Gary Klein.

The premise of these books is that our brains often analyze our circumstances by going through patterns and contexts that we know. Sometimes our brains work so fast that we often don't realize that they are operating at all. Klein tells the story of the fire chief who sensed something wrong in the living room of a burning house, even though the signs of danger were not obvious. However, he was disturbed by the intense heat in the room, even though the flames were small. He ordered his firefighters out, and upon leaving the room, the floor collapsed. The experienced chief had picked up a number of cues and sensed that, below the floor, there was a fire that was burning the support structure. If he had not taken action, all of them would have been lost. (A lifelong friend who happens to be second-in-command in a major metropolitan fire department assured me that this story is accurate.)

Gladwell opens *Blink* with the story of how the J. Paul Getty Museum in California acquired a kouros — a Greek statue of a nude male youth — for nearly $10 million. But soon after it first went on display, an Italian art historian saw the statue and immediately knew it was a fake. The head of the Acropolis Museum in Athens described an "intuitive repulsion" the moment he saw the statue. Upon further investigation, the statue was eventually determined to be a fake, and this truth was uncovered by the immediate and instinctive reactions of experts who knew what they were seeing yet could not articulate it.

All of us can develop such powers of observation, and it is not always necessary to process these cues at computerlike speed. Sometimes the evidence is plainly in front of us, offering glimmers of a hidden truth, just as the crackle in a comb running through our hair is evidence of the phenomenon of static electricity. An astute observer may believe that reduced budgets at her company, along with changes in accounting procedures, may forecast coming financial problems. Noticing new behavior in those close to us may evidence an underlying illness or a problem with substance abuse. When the aides to a government official leave their positions in steady succession, we may await signs of disenchantment with that official's policies.

Research in Action

As I mentioned earlier, my employer transferred me to a defense business in upstate New York in the late 1980s to prepare the employees and the local community for changes in the defense industry. My research provided a glimpse into a more global view of this business, and I was turned this information into a variety of communication media, such as internal newsletters and press releases. The audiences for my messages learned about Americans' growing disaffection for a large Defense Department budget, decreasing world tensions, and increasing competition in the global defense market. These research exercises proved to be a great benefit to me, as I learned that future events are often, perhaps even usually, predictable.

Here's a corollary story with a sadder ending about someone who was ambushed by an unexpected job loss. This man was blinded by the myth of job security even though the signs of change were in full view. The character in this story is Chip, a fictional composite of several people I know who had a similar experience. All had the same avoidable outcome.

Chip graduated high school without definite goals or even a clear sense of self, so he went into the Army. For many people who need to find themselves, the American armed services are a great opportunity. They can provide needed access to training in a new field. Many also use the G.I. Bill of Rights after discharge for post-secondary school education.

Chip got a lot of experience in logistics in the Army, mostly in stocking and distributing materials. After discharge, he got a job with a big corporate retailer managing their storage and distribution.

The company was known for its "employment for life," so he felt secure about his future. They even offered profit sharing, so Chip's life felt nice. He was comfortable enough to marry and raise a son. Once as he was crowing about his security, I mentioned that many corporations were changing their policies, and perhaps his would change, too. I suggested that he might want to take advantage of his educational benefits from the company or from the Army and supplement his skills, just in case anything happened to his position. Angry that I would even suggest such a thing, he responded with indignant steeliness, "I feel I will have a job for life."

Around his fifteenth anniversary, hard times hit the retailer, so they merged with another provider. ("Merger" is a euphemism in this case; Chip's company was acquired). Chip was resentful by what he saw as a betrayal of the compact between him and his employer. His wife reported that, for several days, he went around the house punching the walls and the kitchen cabinets. One of the most difficult aspects to accept about his new employers was that they had their own unique system for handling materials. Chip's training had been in a different, now arcane, methodology, so his skills were not transferable to this new firm. Because he was competing with employees experienced in the new company's ways, Chip was assigned to a different position. He was essentially demoted.

There were other downsides to his new job. The retailer who now employed him was not quite so iconic or as highly regarded as his previous employer had been. Still, it was a local chain of stores with a very loyal customer base. The pay and benefits were only a little less than they were with the bigger company. Also, he still had a job in management, despite its being a bit less prestigious than before. However, this company did seem secure, and it was, for about 10 more years.

After a decade, his new employer downsized him out of the job. Now, with retail stores retrenching across the country, local jobs had become more scarce. Moving was out of the question, as he and his family were firmly planted in their neighborhood. Eventually, Chip found another position with a local, foreign-owned retailer. But, in this position, his role was diminished even further, more of a supervisor than a manager. Soon after the transfer and working in the new job, there were other changes. Raises stopped coming, because sales were flat or declining. Chip's wife went back to work for some extra household money. Worst yet, layoffs were a normal part of life with this company, and he began to lose his co-workers. But Chip was boastful that while others were laid off, he was able to keep his job, diminished as it was from his previous positions. "I must be doing something right," he said.

Eventually, Chip's job was eliminated, too, and he found himself without a job after three decades in the work force. The latest blow seemed to come suddenly, with no warning. Because he was with one employer for years and then transferred to another, he had never really looked for a job, so he had no resume. He had to scramble to get that ready. Still he maintained a positive attitude, saying that perhaps this would be an opportunity to try something new.

Finding "something new" turned out to be not so easy. Chip had trouble getting another job because of a major obstacle he had never envisioned. He was unqualified for any other work despite — or perhaps due to — having more than 30 years of continuous but narrow work experience. He had no college degree because he never took advantage of his educational opportunities. To work in a new occupation would mean starting at the bottom because of his limited work experience and education. Luckily, he found another job in retail, but it came with another cut in pay. As the newest guy, he got the toughest, most strenuous assignments, which were painful for his aging joints.

Over dinner at my house one night, I asked how things were going in the new job. He turned to me and said, "Pat, I never thought I would lose my job. After all, I had worked for more than 30 years."

I found myself incredulous at his response. "How could he have been surprised?" Chip saw his fellow employees laid off over many years, and he witnessed the decline of retail in the United States. Only to myself, I wondered, "Did he think that he was somehow protected, that the laws of economics didn't apply to him?"

Furthermore, Chip never prepared for the possibility that he would lose his job. Through the years, as he aged, he complained that the job was becoming more difficult, yet he never acquired new skills, even though his education would have been free. He never had a resume ready. For all of his years in the workplace, Chip landed in a job that paid him less and was lower in stature than his previous position.

As we peer into an uncertain world with the understanding that change is inevitable, the road ahead may seem dark, perhaps even unknowable. Research helps light the way. It gives us insight into what may lie ahead. We will never be able to predict the future without error or with certainty. However, we can ameliorate our risks by building our base of knowledge and recognizing the sign-posts along the road.

Lessons from Step 3

1. Research on a given subject often supplies clues that can predict upcoming changes.

2. Often the signs of impending change are right before our eyes, if we are open to seeing them.

3. We often do not give ourselves credit for how smart we really are. Many of us should learn to trust our instincts more.

4. Disregarding or not even recognizing the signs of change can prove to be devastating. Ignorance is not bliss; it can prove to be the source of disappointment and long-time regret.

INTERMISSION FOR YOUR TRANSITION

How Far Ahead Can You See?

1. **List the sources of the information and ongoing education that you receive. Once you have done that, number them in priority order.** *(For example, if you receive most of your information from the Internet, that is number one. If you don't have time to read news because you are attending classes, that is your number one.)*

_____

_____

_____

_____

_____

_____

Is television your first source of information? If so, you need to rethink your activities. While TV has its place in how we learn, its very nature reduces material to digestible, shallow bites. Think hard about ways you can expand taking in information. Consider the following:

- At least one general news publication (e.g., *Time, Newsweek, USA Today*)

- At least one business publication (e.g., *Business Week, Fortune, The Wall Street Journal*)

- Books on audio for your car or home

- Local seminars, presentations or speeches

- Courses at your local community college

2. **Inventory all the trends you can see in your local community. Are new businesses being created or are buildings shuttered? Where is employment going? Are new homes of a different quality and value being built?**

_____

_____

_____

_____

_____

_____

_____

3. Examine your own place of work or your own business. What are the trends you see there? Are employees leaving? Are quarterly reports showing higher or lower revenues? Brainstorm them and write them down.

_____

_____

_____

_____

_____

_____

_____

4. Now turn the same critical eye to your own personal situation. Include your family, if you have one. Look at health trends, such as results of check-ups, exercise and amount of medication. What are the trends in work and income? How is your social connectiveness? Do you have many friends, or are you and your family members becoming more isolated?

_____

_____

_____

_____

_____

_____

_____

Keep all this information in mind as we proceed to the next step in our management of change — Proactive Preparation.

> *"It's not the will to win that matters;*
> *everyone has that.*
> *It's the will to prepare to win that matters."*
> — Paul "Bear" Bryant, from his book,
> *"I Ain't Never Been Nothing but a Winner"*

Step 4 — PROACTIVE PREPARATION

Put the pieces in place.

So you accept change as a reality. You know that it is not necessarily positive or negative, but it can be largely shaped by the way you react to it. In fact, you may even have begun to get a sense of changes that are coming down the road. Proactively preparing for change is the next step.

To prepare for change, you first need a strategy —a long-term plan of action designed to achieve a particular goal. The word derives from the Greek *strategos*, which actually comes from two separate words: *stratos* (army) and *ago* (ancient Greek for leading). Formulating a strategy is distinct from putting together tactics or immediate actions. Instead, you should think of it as being *the first step* in your thought process, as strategies help make the problem easier to understand and solve.

The global auto industry is a stunning example of NOT reacting to change and planning in reaction to that change. In the U.S., we easily see the effects of inertia — standing still while all changes around us. As mentioned earlier, the major American carmakers, along with other American car and truck manufacturers were constantly one step behind, like that person in the marching band who is moving at a tempo different from the others. Starting with the 1973 oil embargo, the rest of the world began to learn that oil was a limited resource whose supply could be interrupted at a moment's notice. However, it was a lesson lost in America. Meanwhile, European and Asian carmakers were prepared with smaller, more fuel-efficient vehicles.

When the embargo was over, American automakers and the public continued our old ways. This was an error, exacerbated by the price of gasoline actually declining in the U.S. Instead of learning the value and need for fuel economy, we bought more large vehicles than ever and sales of smaller, more fuel-efficient cars decreased.

Fast forward to the first decade of the 21st century, where we saw oil and gasoline prices rise again, this time much more rapidly. It became too expensive to drive large vehicles, and Americans began to feel higher costs in their pocketbooks. When gasoline hit four dollars per gallon, Americans drove less. They also started driving smaller cars, which were more readily available from non-American carmakers. Hybrid engines — a combination of a traditional internal combustion engine with an electric motor — provided better gas mileage. However, that innovation came from Toyota. They bet big on hybrids, and it paid off.

We mentioned earlier how the term "Big Three" became an anachronism, as Chrysler, Ford and General Motors no longer dominated auto sales. Indeed, as of this writing, auto sales in the U.S. fell nearly 20 percent year-to-year according to a report published in Knowledge@Wharton, an e-newsletter distributed by the Wharton School of Business at the University of Pennsylvania. American car manufacturers are now trying to catch up to their international competitors, such as Toyota, Volkswagen and Nissan. The Americans are cutting overall production of vehicles, particularly those that consume more gasoline. But there is a possibility that their actions are too little, much too late. We will all know better in future editions of this book.

The fact remains that Detroit should have seen this coming, even as far back as 1971. Many popular books on economic trends predicted the rise of both China and India, whose consumption of natural resources has certainly influenced world economies. American carmakers could have retooled their factories over the past four decades. Instead, they have been forced to do it quickly, and perhaps inefficiently, under the circumstances.

Rapid rises and retrenchments in markets don't affect industry alone. We have seen how, in today's global economy, changes in our own employment and small business are a reality. I speak from experience on this. I have been through many changes, and I have been forced to look for new work several times over the course of my career. This was a shock to my father and other men of his generation. In their worlds, they tended to find a job, stay there for 30 or more years, and then collect the pension.

Our own world is different today, yet I remain hopeful. My own experiences have taught me that, though change can be challenging, it is always possible to bounce back. So imagine that you are like that car company facing a rapidly changing world. Picture yourself as your own corporation — (YOUR NAME), Incorporated! As president and CEO and chief marketing officer all rolled into one, take stock of your circumstances, whether you earn a living as an employee of another company, as a small business owner, or as a consultant.

You need to think about who you are serving, whether an employer or a base of customers. What is your mission to the people you serve? If you are saying that you are an accountant or a house painter, then you are probably not thinking creatively or broadly.

I learned this from my grandfather, who worked as a bricklayer. He thought of his work and his service as much more than simply laying one brick atop another. When I was transferred to a different high school, he declared that my new school was an exceptional one.

"Why is that, Grandpop," I asked.

"Because I laid the brick on that school."

He saw himself as more than a bricklayer. He built schools, homes and hospitals.

Similarly, an accountant provides financial services to companies or individuals, finding ways to maximize their financial resources. If you are a house painter, you help homeowners protect their investment against the elements with the right selection of paint. Your craft also provides decoration.

Strengths

A skills inventory is a great opportunity to focus on your capabilities, also called your "transferable skills." What do you bring to the party? What are your strongest capabilities?

Ford Myers, president of Career Potential (www.careerpotential.com), is a superb career counselor who has helped me. An exercise for his clients is called "Passions and Gifts," a series of questions that focuses on these abilities. Here are some of Ford's questions that you can ask yourself to uncover those things that you do well. This self-assessment can also help you define your contribution to an organization:

• *What particularly strong skills do you have?*

• *Of these skills, which show an exceptional ability?*

- *How are you regarded? If your colleagues, friends and acquaintances were asked to describe you, which adjectives would come up most frequently?*

- *What are your greatest contributions to the organizations or groups to which you belong?*

These are good questions to keep in mind throughout the remainder of this book, as awareness of your skills can help you assess your ability to deal with change. Think of the areas in which you can excel. You may be able to use language effectively in expressing yourself artistically or rhetorically. That may cause you to think, "Oh, I've never been a writer, and I never will be." While that may be true when it comes to the poetic or artistic application of language (and you will never really know that until you try), you may be able to apply language in other valuable ways. Those with good language skills are generally adept at reading and writing, telling stories and memorizing text, much as an actor, comedian or other performer will be. Your skills may be persuasive, such as those of sales representatives, fundraisers, lawyers, or those serving public office. You may be instructive, as teachers or counselors are. Language can also be applied in an inspirational way, as a motivational speaker or religious minister may do.

You can see many applications of your unique and varied skills if you look at them imaginatively. Here are some other examples of applicable skills:

- **MATH** — Skills in arithmetic have to do with more than adding or subtracting numbers. These skills may also be used to analyze problems systematically and logically. Where would the business world be without people who could work in accounting, on budgets, and in planning logistical operations? Marketers should be able to project sales and analyze profitability of the products they bring to market. This ability can also be important in recognizing abstract patterns. M.C. Escher, who created idiosyncratic two-dimensional art that looked three-dimensional, owed as much to math as he did to his skills in illustration.

- **MUSICIANSHIP** —It's natural to think automatically of musical skills as only those related to instrumental performance, singing, and composing. However, people with a high level of musical ability also have high aural sensibilities. This makes them sensitive to sounds and tones, along with rhythms. It is not uncommon for people with musical talents to be unable to read music. The great Errol Garner could not read music, yet he was famous as the composer of the classic song, "Misty." He also once reportedly produced an entire album, 40 minutes of music, in a single afternoon simply by sitting in a studio and improvising.

  I have such familiarity with music. I sing with a large *a cappella* group and have played several instruments in my life, even though I also don't read music particularly well. However, with whatever modest musical skills I have, they have manifested themselves in my video and film career, especially when the time came to pick background music for my productions. In another way, these skills likely contributed to my ability to write speeches, audio-visual scripts, and auditory works (i.e., writing for the ear rather than the eye or the written page.) Musical intelligence can be found among the very spiritual, and it may contribute to a graceful and rhythmic way of speaking. It's obvious that musical skills may lead to playing, singing, and composing, but they may also lead some to be disk jockeys, recording technicians, and managers in the music business.

- **PHYSICALITY** — This is the ability to use one's body, in movement or other action, to provide solutions. Activities like sports, dancing or acting come to mind. Physical skills are also important in such areas as building and crafts. One of my high school classmates is a successful surgeon, and he maintains the manual skills needed in the operating room by woodworking.

- **SPATIAL RECOGNITION** — This skill leads one to identify and use the patterns of space. It may aid in "sensing" the distance between objects, like the craftsman who can look at an open area and cut just the right length of material to fill it, such as a piece of wood or a pipe. People with strong spatial recognition may be good at visualizing the placement of objects, just as a good interior designer knows exactly where to place a chair or table in a room. Those with spatial recognition may also have that mystical "sense of direction," a skill needed by a guide, a hunter, or a cartographer. Other ideal careers for those with this skill include artists, engineers, and architects.

- **SOCIAL SKILLS** — Did you ever meet people whom everyone seems to like? These men and women seem to have the uncanny ability to see into the souls of others and feel empathy for them. They understand the inner desires and motivating forces of the people they meet. People like these have high social skills. They are usually extroverts, and they are known for their ability to work well in a group. They communicate well, as they understand the wants and needs of the people with whom they are speaking, They tend to enjoy a healthy discussion, though they are careful not to cross over the line into argument, because that would be off-putting to those around them. Careers well suited to people with highly developed social skills include politicians, managers of people, teachers and instructors, and, especially, diplomats.

- **INTROSPECTION/SELF-REFLECTION** — While this is probably the most nebulous characteristic I have come across in my research, it manifests itself in tangible ways. This is the capacity to understand one's own self-worth and ability to contribute. People with this ability are usually highly self-aware. They know what makes them "tick." This ability to self-assess can help the recognition of one's own accomplishments, a vital part of making plans and setting goals. The top performers in their respective fields tend to have this trait. When you are tuned into yourself, you know who you are. You know what you CAN do and what you WANT to do. You know how you react to your conditions, so you know which conditions you should avoid. Conversely, you recognize opportunities on which you should capitalize. Just as we are attracted to people with outward social skills, we tend also to be attracted to those who are self-knowing and introspective. We admire (perhaps even covet) their confidence, self-direction, determination, and drive. They have a strong sense of identity and purpose. People with these qualities tend to be philosophical. Good jobs for these people are psychologists, theologians, police officers, politicians, and religious ministers.

So, it is time to take a skills inventory based on the areas noted above. Take a tablet of paper and brainstorm a list of all the things you do well. Ask yourself as many rhetorical questions as you can imagine, such as:

• How are my language skills? How clearly do I express myself? Typically, how well do I get my point across to others?

• How well can I instruct others on a task that I know well but which is new to them?

• How are my physical skills? How well can I lift or carry objects?

• How is my eye-to-hand coordination? How well could I handle tools if necessary?

• How adept am I with numbers? How well could I estimate

the costs of a project? What is my ability to create a project or departmental budget and manage it?

- How may my aural and listening skills contribute to my work? Do I hear and listen well, catching not only the details in what is said to me but also the nuances?

- How would I describe my visual skills? How well do I arrange objects? Are they visually pleasing when I am finished? Do I have a sense of size and distance, enabling me to estimate physical materials that are needed?

- What motivates me? What are the tasks on the job that will energize me, and which will disinterest me? How determined am I to "get the job done?"

- How often do I set goals? How well do I set them? And once I set goals, how effective am I in *fulfilling* them?

- What are my social skills like? Can I empathize with the wants and needs of my colleagues?

- How well do I handle the inevitable differences of opinion? Can people work with me? Do people even want to work with me?

- How well do I motivate or inspire others to action? How adept am I in determining the wants and needs of others and then addressing them?

You could probably devise more questions. The point of this exercise is to stimulate self-knowledge — an honest assessment of your skills. Knowing just what you offer will begin to help you understand where (YOUR NAME), Incorporated can best contribute to others.

Weaknesses

Of course, this is the converse of the questions above. Which skills do you particularly *lack*? Of all the things for which you are known, which abilities are noticeably absent? This is the time to leave your ego aside and give up the pretense that you can do it all. After all, none of us can, not even the best of us. Norman Vincent Peale, known internationally as the quintessential positive thinker, advised that you should also have a "humble but reasonable confidence in your own powers." Without both sides of that equation, you cannot be successful or happy.

For example, if you were to look at yourself honestly, could you admit that you become tongue-tied under pressure, or are given to misuses of language when speaking publicly? If so, that's okay. Not all of us can be great orators. But you should also face up to the fact that you are probably not the right choice to be the company spokesperson!

Similarly, there are basic math skills that are essential to work. The supervisors on construction assignments may not be the chief financial officers of their companies, but they need to know how to calculate the amount of material needed to complete a job and its cost. (I was amused once when a co-worker heard that I was going to college part-time to attain an advanced degree in business. She disparaged my particular program because there was such a heavy emphasis on math. I pointed out that since the program would lead me to a master of business administration degree, I needed to understand accounting, budgeting, economics and statistics… you know, disciplines that are germane to running a business! Her attitude was analogous to one who aspired to a master's degree in creative writing, but didn't want to bother learning how to punctuate a sentence.)

Similarly, you need to address your softer skills: your ability to work with others, your ability to plan and then execute that plan to its completion. Consider also the ability to negotiate not only with vendors, but also with members of your own organization. What do you know about dealing with sudden, unexpected challenges?

Continue your skills inventory and determine areas in which you are less competent. Determine if these areas will prevent you from doing your job well. If so, how well or how easily can you learn new skills or improve the ones you have? (I stopped playing pick-up basketball years ago because I had to admit that, even if I were coached by Michael Jordan himself, I would only embarrass myself. In the workplace, I could not begin to run a production operation because I have no understanding of the mechanical processes. And, I hire people to perform nearly all the maintenance on my house because I am simply dangerous with tools.)

If you are not skilled in certain areas, how easily can you delegate them to others, given your place in the organization? A head of a finance operation may be a whiz at forecasting, but she may choose to hire an expert to handle taxes. Similarly, the chiefs of hospital staffs employ a wide range of medical specialists in their institutions. They are not expected to know all the specialties themselves.

As with your strengths, knowing your weaknesses is all part of the plan for (YOUR NAME), Incorporated. It is another part of an honest assessment of your overall value.

Opportunities

Opportunities are external factors, and the most successful among us tend to be able to recognize them and then exploit them. Opportunities may come in the form of evolving trends in the marketplace or society. Stock trading, an activity once reserved for the well-heeled, became available to the middle class through online services that charge reduced fees. Many entrepreneurs saw opportunity in the growth of two-income households, as businesses and service sprang up to serve families whose time was stretched. Now people can employ childcare workers, home organizers, even dog walkers. Others saw opportunities in the Internet and used it as a new kind of storefront to sell products as varied as pet food, hot sauces, and monocles. Of course, there is also the online bazaar called eBay®.

Opportunities may come in the form of new international markets. For example, as the middle class grows in China and India, they create a brand new venue for automobiles. Who will serve those needs effectively? Which automaker will offer those buyers the features they want at the most attractive price point?

Sam Walton was successful by serving the retail market more effectively than his competitors did. Mr. Walton found ways to keep his prices lower, and that enabled Wal-Mart to thrive and win in a retail market that many others had once ruled, most notably Sears. Today, Wal-Mart operates around the world, in countries as far-flung as the United Kingdom, Mexico, Japan, Argentina, Brazil and Canada.

There are notable miscalculations, too. As mentioned earlier, the American auto industry learned *TWICE* that there was market potential for fuel-efficient cars — once in the early 1970s and then again in the early 21st century. Both times, they chose to concentrate on the larger profits of larger vehicles and trucks. The result is that, as of this writing, the financial stability of the Detroit Three is highly questionable. They did not exploit the opportunities facing them as oil became more scarce and more expensive.

So as you survey your own landscape, where are your opportunities? Consider the following examples:

- What are your unique skills that earn you a special niche where you can serve? Are you one of a dwindling number of auto mechanics able to work on older engines? If so, you may be an asset to owners of vintage cars. Do you have a craft that is disappearing, such as stone masonry, calligraphy, even hand embroidery?

- Do you have a unique capability to serve your company as it moves into new areas? Perhaps you are more familiar than others are with a new industry. Perhaps your firm has entered healthcare, and you were once a nurse or other caregiver. If your workplace has entered the defense industry, perhaps you have background in the military that can be brought to bear.

- You may notice that there is an influx of a certain ethnic group in your locality. Are you familiar with these people? Do you understand their culture? Can you speak their language? Perhaps you can serve them with a restaurant that offers the cuisine they prefer.

Threats

While opportunities certainly affect our worlds, threats are also external factors that can derail our plans. They may come in many forms. In our businesses, a common threat may be the entrance of a new competitor. Perhaps there is a change in pricing structures that risks your competitiveness, such as in the cost of materials or labor. Perhaps there is a new tax imposed by a governing body on your particular product or service.

On the other hand, changes may happen to you personally rather than in your business or employment. Perhaps there is a change in your health that requires you to be out of the office more often or changes your physical abilities. Your industry may have introduced a new technology that gives you new capabilities or shortens your business processing time. Are you up on these changes?

Look at your industry and your market. Examine what your competition is doing (and "competition" includes individuals who do your job as well as other companies).

Look at the specifications that are generally required for your job, products, or services. Look also at the technology associated with your company or your position. Are your knowledge and skills up-to-date? Many people I knew in the printing industry had to retool when the industry went from a film-based method of distribution to electronic files. I have worked with many communicators who were on the leading edge of technology with video production. Now much of that same type of communications is accomplished through the Internet, requiring not only different skills but also a different sensitivity to the unique aesthetics of the medium.

Sometimes threats are not external. Review your set of weaknesses. Could any of them seriously threaten your business or your position? If so, you could think of classes or seminars to shore up those areas that need improvement. I recently attended a seminar on the newest Internet technologies. Another participant was a man in his late 70s who was truly a legend in local advertising. Even though he could just as easily have delegated the seminar to another person in his agency, or hired someone with the talent, he sought to keep himself vital by continuing to learn and grow. This attitude is probably one of the reasons he was such a leader in his industry.

The proactive preparation for change is a bigger part of our lives than we realize, if we are conscientious. Think of the ways you are already prepared for change in your personal life, practicing responsibility without even thinking about it. Do you have insurance for your home, your car, and your life? Do you have a will? Beyond your will, have you written down your advanced directives, your so-called "living will?" Most of us do these things because we know they are dutiful courses of actions for the people to whom we are dependable.

However, we sometimes do not go far enough in our planning. For example, if you lost your job tomorrow, how would you pay your bills? Most financial advisers say we should all have three months of salary saved for an emergency. I used to overlook that advice. Today I have that money set aside in addition to an open line of credit that will help me access more money, if I need it.

Would you be prepared to start looking for a new job tomorrow if you lost your current job today? I am always surprised when layoffs happen in an organization and people turn and say, "I guess I should get my resume in order." *You should ALWAYS have your resume in order!* You never know when your job situation may change. And even if your employment is stable, you never know when that recruiter will call with the job of a lifetime. What would the recruiters on the other end of the line think of you if they called, offering you the opportunity you have been waiting for, and you said, "It sounds great. I'll send my resume when it's ready." You may just go to the bottom of their wish list.

People who work for others for a living must understand that they can move their employment from one organization to another if their skills are transferable. The more specific your skills, the more specific and limited the slots you can fill. As you broaden your skills, so do you expand your range of job opportunities.

But preparing for change means more than assessing and upgrading our skill sets. We must also learn to apply our talents to the world as it truly exists. The ability to look over the horizon and recognize reality is the gift of vision. A notable example of such a vision came from Chuck Geschke and John Warnock, who worked to-gether at Xerox Corporation's research center. Geschke and Warnock recognized that there was a need to bring print production in house rather than rely entirely on external print companies, so they created electronic document software. Xerox's management loved what Geschke and Warnock had made, so the two men traveled to corporate headquarters to discuss a marketing rollout of this new product. But according to Geschke, management said the plan would have to wait. It seemed that Xerox normally spent seven years to launch a new product.

Geschke said that this sort of delay was insane. In the fast-moving world of computer technology, seven years was equal to several generations. By the time the product hit the market, he argued, it would already be out-of-date. The response from management was that they were sorry, but that was how long it took at Xerox — seven years. So Geschke and Warnock took their idea and in 1982 created Adobe Systems, a leader in electronic print production. They recognized the need for electronic document files in a changing world. They seized their opportunity and applied their skills to it. Today Adobe is one of the ten largest software companies in the world with major development operations in the U.S., Canada, Germany, India, and Romania.

Philosopher and longshoreman Eric Hoffer once said, "In times of change, learners inherit the Earth, while the learned find themselves beautifully equipped to deal with a world that no longer exists." I interpret this to mean that, once we consider ourselves among the "learned," we are in danger of becoming complacent and closing ourselves off to new information about the world as it really is. But if we remain lifelong learners, we are more likely to be prepared for many of the changes we will face.

LESSONS FROM STEP 4

1. Formulating a strategy is the first step in your thought process as you prepare for change. It precedes a plan and tactics.

2. In order to envision yourself in the midst of change, picture yourself as your own corporation — (YOUR NAME), Incorporated. Think of yourself as an organization with a mission, a market, and a profit center.

3. In order to know how we compete, we must assess ourselves honestly and thoroughly. What are our strengths? What do we offer others?

   What may be our weaknesses, the areas in which we can't compete with others?

   What opportunities lie ahead of us? Are there societal or market changes ahead on which we can capitalize?

   What are the threats we may face? Do we face personal change, such as a new health situation or an oncoming debt? Are there market changes on the horizon, such as a technological change that will render our product or services out-of-date?

4. Author Jonathan Swift once said, "Vision is the art of seeing things invisible." It is important to recognize the world as it really is, not the way we wish to see it.

Intermission For Your Transition

Time to Get Ready.

1. Let's examine "(YOUR NAME), Incorporated." Review yourself and your situation, whether you are an employee, a small business owner, or an independent worker. (This last category may range anywhere from a consultant to a freelance writer, or as a plumber for hire, or as a nurse contracting your services.) *What is your mission? What do you offer your customers or employers? You may recognize this in the form of a job description or the stated purpose of your company. Try to think more broadly of your special gifts. Be imaginative.*

_____

_____

_____

_____

_____

_____

_____

Who do you serve?

_____

_____

_____

_____

_____

What sets you apart and distinguishes you from others who do the same work you do?

_____

_____

_____

_____

_____

2. **Inventory your strengths. What particularly strong skills do you have?**

_____

_____

_____

_____

_____

What are the unique gifts and qualities for which you are known?

_____

_____

_____

_____

_____

3. Turn the same introspective eye to your weaknesses. What are the areas in which you are less competent?

_____

_____

_____

_____

_____

How can you learn to obtain new skills or improve your weaker abilities?

_____

_____

_____

_____

_____

4. What are the external factors that you may be able to exploit as opportunities? What are the societal or market changes and trends that you may be able to exploit? *For example, is there a burgeoning technology in which you are an expert? Are new citizens entering your community with needs that you are particularly able to fulfill?*

_____

_____

_____

_____

_____

5. On the flip side of opportunities, are there threats that may be awaiting you? What are the societal or market changes and trends that may diminish what you have to offer your customers or your employer?

_____

_____

_____

_____

_____

6. Given all the factors listed above, list the things that you can do to make the most of your best abilities. Also, list activities that can improve those areas in which you are less proficient.

_____

_____

_____

_____

_____

_____

_____

_____

_____

_____

_____

_____

_____

> *"Think before you act."*
> — Aesop, legendary Greek fabulist,
> in his story, *"The Fox and the Hound"*

Step 5 — PLANNING

Map out your campaign.

Aesop advised us of the importance of planning millennia ago. And so it is, still today. Once you have identified the change that is either happening to you or the change that you will cause to happen, you need a plan of action. A plan serves three important purposes:

- It helps to focus the activities on the tasks needed to fulfill the stated goals.

- It creates a structure and an agenda under which the identified tasks can be performed.

- It creates targets in order that the performance can be evaluated.

A well-prepared plan demonstrates that you know where you're going, how you will get there, and whether or not you have truly arrived. By deciding in advance what you want to do, how you will do it, and when to do it, the future becomes more knowable. I cannot guarantee that a plan will cause you to succeed in your endeavors, but I can almost guarantee that the *lack* of a plan will deliver failure and disappointment.

Effective plans consist of three basic elements:

1. **Goals**, or objectives, refer to those things that you want to achieve and when you want to achieve them. Goal development

is the first integral part of strategy formation. Without goals, we cannot go forward. It is like starting out on a vacation and driving the highways without a destination in mind. Your objectives must be clear. They should be measurable so it is apparent when the goal has been achieved. Here are some examples that can touch us both on the job and in our personal lives:

Not measurable: "I want a raise in salary."
Measurable: "I want to raise my salary by at least ten percent each year.

Not measurable: "We must reduce our department's expenditures over the next year."
Measurable: "We must reduce our department's expenditures by 20 percent over the next year."

Not measurable: "I must lose weight."
Measurable: "I will lose (this much) weight," or "I will reduce my waist by (a certain measurement)."

Not measurable: "I will help my child be a good reader in school."
Measurable: "I will help my child achieve a 10-year-old reading level at age 8."

Goals should also be realistic. It is not reasonable to expect that you can double your $50,000 annual salary with one promotion. It is also not realistic (or desirable) to lose 50 pounds in a month. Such unrealistic and unattainable goals set you up for disappointment, and they will lead to the abandonment of achievement, as you tell yourself, "I can't do that! Why should I even bother?"

2. **Tactics** must be formulated. They are the individual steps you will take to meet your goals, as noted above. For example, when I was in charge of marketing for a large regional hospital,

my goal was to increase participation in our community health seminars, which not only served the public, but also raised the overall awareness of the hospital. My tactics included the following:

- **Studying the demographics of our community to determine patients' most likely needs.** This hospital marketed actively to maternity patients, yet the local population was aging. When I aimed the marketing towards geriatric patients and presented seminars on orthopedics and giving care to those suffering from Alzheimer's disease, attendance shot up.

- **Advertising more aggressively through direct mail.** Newspaper readership was declining. We raised the response rate by putting the information directly into the attendees' hands and by sending easy-to-read materials directly to their homes.

- **Conducting active feedback at the end of every session.** We found new topics in which there was interest by asking the attendees directly, rather than presenting seminars on those procedures that we wanted to push.

NOTE: A tactic should not be confused with a strategy, which is the entire design for managing a situation or event effectively. While a strategy is broadly based, tactics are detailed.

Many people are tactical without being strategic. Such people are able to put together a list of things to do over the next few days, every month, perhaps even over the coming year. An example may be the logistics manager who knows how to find the cheapest and fastest ways to ship a product but hasn't set a goal of improving *all* logistics, defined as the procurement, distribution, maintenance and replacement of materials.

Such people don't sit high enough in the mast of their personal ships; therefore, they cannot see beyond their current view. These people often work feverishly, accomplishing little, and confusing *motion* with *direction*.

3. **Schedules** set an appropriate sense of realistic urgency to a plan, just as the goals must be realistically attainable, as noted above. Schedules can come in a wide variety of timeframes — long range, intermediate range, or short range. An unrealistically short timeframe can breed disillusionment, but an extended deadline may create lethargy, preventing you from reaching the goal at all.

Though it may not appear specifically in your plan, remember to consider *flexibility* — built-in buffers and contingencies for the unpredictable or unknowable factors that may arise. For example, your goal to learn to play a certain musical piece on the piano may be delayed by an illness. Yet, you may choose to use that downtime to review musical theory or the notes and tempo of the piece you are learning. Such attention will help you recover from unexpected distractions like these.

So, you may be wondering about the relevance of planning in your own day-to-day life. "Oh, I don't need to put a formal plan together. I just know what I want to do, and I'll just go ahead and do it." Consider instead some ordinary events that you may need to handle. Are any of these as simple as "just doing it?"

Planning a Birthday Party

What is there to planning a party? Just get some snacks, drinks, and cake, tell everyone when to arrive, and it will take care of itself! Then again, here are some considerations.

How many people are coming? If you don't know that, how big a space will you need? Is your home sufficient, or must you rent a space? Who is coming? Is it a children's party or a party for an adult? That means very different menus.

What kind of food *will* you serve? Are snacks sufficient, or will the party be held over lunchtime or dinnertime? Your decision depends on who will be invited and how many will come.

By the way, is this a surprise party? Is a surprise party even appropriate? Maybe not, if the celebrant is your 90-year-old grandmother with a heart condition. You may not want a group of people jumping out and yelling her name. But then again, what's the big deal? It's only a birthday party. Isn't it?

Remodeling Your Home

What is the purpose of the remodeling? Are you merely enlarging an existing space, such as building an addition to your living room, or are you repurposing it altogether (e.g., turning that extra bedroom into a media room)? If so, what are the construction considerations? Will the contractor merely lay a concrete foundation or build out some walls? Perhaps you want to remove an interior wall to make a room larger. Is the interior wall a load-bearing wall that will require reinforcement? How long can you afford to have the contractor disrupting your home? Do you need this job to be completed by a certain date? And how much can you afford? How much can you afford in overages if weather delays the project?

Planning for a Medical Procedure

You need to have an operation that will require some time to recuperate at home. No problem, you're a pretty healthy person, and you can take care of yourself. But what will be your condition afterwards? Can you go up and down the stairs on your own?

Doing so may not be advisable if you're receiving certain types of medication.

Wait, what kind of medication will you actually require after the procedure? What are the side effects? Will it affect your judgment? How may it affect your ability to feed or bathe yourself? Do you need someone to be with you around the clock? If so, who is available? Perhaps you cannot presume that your significant other is available because his or her employer is not that flexible.

The point is that many things are not as simple as they may seem at first. Once you begin handling situations like these and many others, you can be sure that you will soon be working with a tablet of paper to figure out all the variables, coordinate schedules, and try to predict contingencies. Again, planning will help lead to a much happier outcome than if you had left these conditions to chance .

Writing a Plan

Many notable minds have considered planning throughout history. Military strategists in particular continue to influence our strategies today. For example, scan the bookshelves of most executive offices in the United States, and you are bound to find a copy of *The Art of War* by Sun Tzu. Even though it was written in the 6th century B.C., this iconic book is generally regarded as the definitive work on military strategies and tactics. The premises of *The Art of War* and other books on the military continue to sway us. For example, most marketing terms relate to the military, such as *campaign*, which derives from the French word for "military expedition."

In all this time, I don't believe that anyone has come up with the perfect, one-size-fits-all template for a plan. In fact, in all the plans that I have created over the years — whether they have been for video productions, internal communication, crisis communications, and more — I haven't used the exact same format more than once. However, it is most important to remember that any plan contain the three basic elements: goals, tactics, and schedules. I will present one format that I have used as a simple example and guide. You can find many others through a search on the Internet. Better yet, you probably will be able to design your own through practice and experience.

Action Plan for _____

Goal

Strategy

Action to be Taken	Person(s) Responsible	Deadline	Resources Needed?
1.	1.	1.	1.
2.	2.	2.	2.
3.	3.	3.	3.
4.	4.	4.	4.
5.	5.	5.	5.

Measurement (How will you know whether or not you have succeeded?)

Here are two examples of planning that I would like to share with you. One involves a man whose career was all but dead while the other is a simpler story about an ordinary man who wanted to make his final plans. Both are ultimately success stories.

A RETURN TO THE GOOD LIFE

As a professional marketer, I have planned many campaigns, so I believe I can judge success pretty well. One marketer who I admire is someone named D'Andrea Benedetto. He's the son of a musician and painter named Anthony Dominick Benedetto. D'Andrea is better known as Danny Bennett, and his father is singer Tony Bennett.

I also admire the senior Mr. Bennett, who is generally considered one of the best singers of the 20th and 21st centuries. However, in researching his life through several sources, including magazine articles, online postings, and his autobiography, one common truth emerges: we are lucky to have Tony Bennett with us today. While he had great artistic and commercial success in the 1950s and 1960s, his brand of music eventually fell out of style when it was overtaken by rock-and-roll. By the end of the 70s, Mr. Bennett had no recording contract, no manager, and no concerts outside of Las Vegas. He had a $2 million tax debt, and the Internal Revenue Service wanted to take his Los Angeles home. By his own admission, he was abusing marijuana and cocaine. When he got news of the IRS's actions against him, Mr. Bennett "overindulged" (his term, as stated in his autobiography, *"The Good Life"*), and he was rushed to the hospital. It was then he called Danny for help.

Mr. Bennett lamented to his son that the public was just not interested in his particular music anymore. While Danny was an aspiring rock-and-roll musician, he was also involved in the business of selling music. His father was a mirror image of Danny

— a tremendous musical talent who didn't have the skills to administer his career. Recognizing the predicament, Danny became his father's manager. His plan was NOT to change his father's performance style; after all, that was what he did best. Instead, Danny made his father's music desirable again, this time to a younger audience.

First, Danny helped get his father's finances under control, putting him on a strict budget. Then Danny moved his father back to New York and into a small Manhattan apartment. He booked him in smaller, different venues, veering him away from the Las Vegas image. Soon, Mr. Bennett was performing at colleges and small theaters. In the mid-1980s, Danny even managed to get his father a new contract with Columbia Records. His next album became his first to reach the charts in almost 15 years.

Thanks to Danny, Mr. Bennett's "hip" quotient was going way up with appearances on "The Simpsons," and MTV. Tony Bennett was becoming cool again, and his redefining moment came in 1994 when he appeared on MTV's "Unplugged" program, a venue generally reserved for current artists. The CD of the show was named "Album of the Year," receiving a Grammy®, the American recording industry's highest award.

It would not be accurate to say that Tony Bennett had arrived or that he came back. The image Danny projected was that his father never went away in the first place. Young people liked the music they were hearing. As Danny put it, "To them, it was different. If you're different, you stand out."

Since his career was reborn, Tony Bennett has won at least a dozen more Grammys and two Emmys. He was honored by the Kennedy Center for his contribution to the performing arts, was elected to several "halls of fame," and even had one of his paintings put on permanent display in Washington, DC. This all came to a man who nearly died 30 years before.

Pop's Plan

I got the news from one of my brothers on Valentine's Day. Our father, Mario Rocchi, was diagnosed with liver cancer after suffering from what we all thought was the flu. While there were frantic efforts at first to put him on a donor list for a new liver, that possibility was soon abandoned when his doctors came to realize the grim reality — this was a serious disease that was likely to overtake him in about ten months.

Pop was never one to waste time. He vowed that he was not simply going to roll over for this disease. Our family lived close to one of the leading cancer centers in the U.S. We also had the good fortune that my brother's wife was a critical care nurse there. With her guidance, Pop would learn which treatments were best for him.

Running parallel to his goal of survival were the practical considerations of what to do if he succumbed to the disease. This concern showed the other side of Pop's personality, that of a responsible and loving husband and patriarch. With the precision of the engineer he was, he made his arrangements. He spelled out where his belongings would go. He wanted me to have a special watch with diamond insets. One brother got a special key ring that was instantly identifiable by a lucky coin imbedded in the middle. My brother-in-law would get the ring that marked Pop's service with his long-time employer. And so it went, with each item and its recipient marked on a long piece of paper in the elegant cursive style that he developed by hand-lettering blueprints for 60 years.

For a while, it seemed that Pop got a reprieve when his cancer simply stopped growing. His oncologist held the pads of her thumb and index finger together and said, "Mario, your tumor could fit in there. And as long as it is that small, we will adopt a practice of watchful waiting."

The ten-month diagnosis stretched on for another ten months. Pop went on with his life, understanding that each day was a gift. Then one day, he couldn't escape or explain the itching on his abdomen. It was a sign that the cancer had started growing, and now it had manifested itself outside his abdomen, on his stomach.

One day, Pop's doctors advised him that they could do no more for him. We arranged for him to come home to hospice care. And early on a November morning, 22 months after his first diagnosis, one year past the original prognosis, Pop quietly passed.

After the undertakers came to take Pop's body, we spared our mother the continued burden of seeing her home as a hospital room. We quickly disassembled Pop's hospital bed, put the sofa and chairs back in their rightful places, and restored the living room to the way it was before hospice. We then read a letter that Pop had written for us five and a half years earlier, well before he was diagnosed with cancer. Though he was gone, his caring and humor came through clearly :

> Dear Rita and All My Children:
>
> If you are reading this, I have passed on, so you should have my will and insurance papers.
>
> Contact (my former employer)... Mom will be entitled to my pension for her lifetime, which I have been paying for out of my retirement pension. This will be in addition to any Social Security she may receive...

Funeral arrangements can be as follows — A viewing the night before with just enough flowers so not to be too miserly. A rosary in my hands is nice. If you so desire rings on my fingers for viewing, fine, but remove them before closing the casket. Leave the rosary!

If you agree to a one-day funeral, fine, just do it. If my grandchildren can be my pallbearers, this would be nice. Say nice things about me, even if they aren't true.

After the burial, have a nice meal out, then return home and enjoy a period together.

I hope you mourn me because you hate to see me leave, not for any guilty feeling, because I don't feel any of you should have this feeling... I'm very happy and proud to have been called "Pop" by each one of you. God has been very good to Mom and me, to have given us charge of such wonderful, loving children.

To my wife, I leave hopefully as friend, lover and real soul mate because you have been all of that to me!!! My life with you has been wonderful to say the least... We have always respected and cared for each other... You have always been there for me, and I hope I was always there for you. I certainly hope the best for you always!

To my children again — Do me and your mother **proud.** I will be watching!!

Mario D. Rocchi

Both Danny Benedetto and Pop stand as shining examples of people who took care of their loved ones' needs through detailed and thoughtful planning. I share my father's personal letter as an example of one ordinary man's realization of his end goals, first by laying out a plan and then bringing them to fruition through faithful, focused execution. He wanted my mother to have financial security, so he arranged for that in his pension, sacrificing some of the initial payout in exchange for her long-term benefit. She never had to worry about that — Pop simply took care of it. He also made his final wishes known, and, despite whatever our opinions may have been, we knew what he wanted to wear, what he wanted to remain in his casket, what music to play at the church, and which details were up to our discretion.

Similarly, Danny DeBenedetto looked after his father's needs. Thanks to Danny, Tony Bennett staged a remarkable ascendancy in his autumnal years, despite seemingly daunting change. This outcome did not simply happen for Tony. It was the result of an imaginative and carefully structured plan. Doesn't it make you wonder what any of us are capable of accomplishing throughout our lives, provided our health holds up and we don't give up?

So, what are your plans to make change happen? The recommendations above are broad but applicable, achievable, and adaptable to your needs with some imagination. Think of all you can do for yourself, for others, and in your workplace.

Once you have such a plan, we head to our last P, which will help you put it into action.

LESSONS FROM STEP 5

1. Either in order *to make change happen* or *to deal with the changes thrust upon you*, you need a plan. If you improvise, you leave too much to chance.

2. An effective plan consists of four basic elements:

    a. Goals, or objectives, that are measurable

    b. Tactics that provide a pathway to the specific action items you will accomplish

    c. Schedules, to add an appropriate sense of urgency

    d. Flexibility, to account for the unknowable

3. What you want to accomplish may seem simple at first. However, you will come to realize that you need to account for the variables that are involved.

Intermission For Your Transition

Use Your Head; Plan Ahead.

1. Now that you have identified change that you are facing now,
   or will face imminently, list measurable goals that will help
   you manage these challenges. *(Refer back to the text in this
   chapter to review how to write a measurable goal, which will allow
   you to set reasonable expectations and an identifiable level of
   achievement.)*

_____

_____

_____

_____

_____

_____

_____

2. What must you do to accomplish the goals listed above? Brainstorm them, considering all possibilities.

_____

_____

_____

_____

_____

_____

3. What is a realistic timeframe for completing the tactics that you have listed? Be realistic; find that balance between "insufficiently urgent" and "overly ambitious."

_____

_____

_____

_____

_____

_____

4. Take one last look at these tactics and the time you have given yourself to accomplish them. Now imagine the contingencies — the possible, unforeseen conditions that may impede your progress. How would you handle them if they occurred in the course of your plan?

_____

_____

_____

_____

_____

5. Transfer all the information you have listed in Steps 1 through 4 into an action plan template. Either use the one shown in this chapter or create one of your own. In any case, make sure that it shows your goals, the tactics you will use to accomplish these goals, and a schedule or deadline for accomplishing them. *(Feel free to add any other elements that will make the plan more relevant to your needs or your style.)*

_____

_____

_____

_____

_____

> *"Decide what you want,*
> *decide what you are willing to exchange for it.*
> *Establish your priorities and go to work."*
> — American Oil Man H. L. Hunt

Step 6 — PERFORMANCE

It is time to execute, or you will be executed by change.

The only thing worth less than a discarded piece of blank paper is the discarded plan that never came to be. Now that you have learned the importance of setting goals and devised a plan to do so, you must execute it with precision and persistence. Mr. Lawrence Bossidy, a CEO who is credited with turning around two major U.S. corporations, co-authored a book simply titled *Execution*. He noticed that there were many books about planning and vision but none about executing. He said in an interview, "The key to change …is having an execution discipline. Having an execution discipline is about getting the job done, to be sure, but with a broad systematic view — one that integrates the mission objective with the tools, the metrics, the people, and the processes that will get you there."

I agree. It is not enough to dream or imagine. No feel-good sayings in the world will turn your dreams to realities. The skills that I have outlined for you so far in this book are important for re-imagining the future. However, I am painfully aware of the shortage of such abilities, whether we are looking in a corporation, a social club, or within a family. Having spent my career in the corporate world, I have seen more than my share of highly degreed managers who know how to spout business theories but could not run a mail room if they needed to do so.

According to an article in the Knowledge@Wharton newsletter, such a shortage of skills in execution can have serious consequences. In a survey of senior executives at 197 companies conducted by a management consulting firm, Marakon Associates and the Economist Intelligence Unit, respondents said their firms achieved only 63 percent of the expected results of their strategic plans. That is less than two thirds. Michael Mankins, a managing partner in Marakon's San Francisco office, says he believes much of that gap between expectation and performance comes from a failure to execute the company's strategy effectively.

This is the point in the Six P's where you must develop the skill set to execute your plan, using your objectives as the milestones that will measure your advancement to success — as you have defined it. In the end, the only true measurement of the fulfillment of your objectives is *effectiveness.* You must ask yourself if you actually *did* what you *set out to do.* If your goal was to lose at least 10 pounds, did you do lose *at least* 10 pounds? Not nine or eight, but 10? If your goal at work was to increase your business margins to 15 percent or more, did you reach that goal? While it may sound harsh, you did not succeed in reaching your goal if your margins were 14 percent or less.

Not only must you deliver on your goals, but you must also choose the right goals. For example, it might be possible that losing 10 pounds was not the right goal. Perhaps you need to lose enough weight and exercise sufficiently to reduce your blood pressure. (I speak from experience here. I manage Type 2 diabetes, and my goal is to attain a certain score in a blood test that I take every three months. If I keep that score in a certain range, then my risk of complications from the diabetes is minimized.) Or perhaps increasing your target margin of 15 percent was too low, too modest a goal because the average margin in your industry is upwards of 20 percent. Below that, you are not achieving the operational efficiencies you should. So discuss your goals with whomever you need to — your physician, your accountant, your chief of information technology — in order to determine if your goals are the right ones.

When we begin to excuse or rationalize our less-than-successful efforts, we are on the unstable and dangerous precipice of making such shortcomings *a habit*. If it was okay to miss this goal, then what about the next one? And then the one after that? Here are some notable misses and their consequences.

• According to the website of the National Highway Traffic Safety Administration, the U.S. Congress sets the Corporate Average Fuel Economy (CAFE) for automakers. CAFE is the average fuel economy, expressed in miles per gallon (mpg), of a manufacturer's fleet of passenger cars or light trucks. CAFE applies to vehicles with a gross weight of 8,500 lbs. or less, manufactured for sale in the United States, for any given model year. "Fuel economy" is defined as the average mileage traveled by an automobile per gallon of gas, measured according to protocols set by the Environmental Protection Agency (EPA).

Many years ago, the EPA set a goal — double the 1974 fuel economy average for passenger cars to 27.5 mpg by 1985. However, these standards were lowered between 1986 and 1989, until the standard of 27.5 mpg was set again in 1990, where it has remained ever since. So a standard set for 1985 was not met in time, and it remains unmet today, decades later. Imagine how much more competitive the American car industry would have been had the CAFE standard been met on time. Instead, Americans who want better gas mileage have turned to autos made outside the country. (Compare this to the success of Toyota's hybrid auto, the Prius, which was successfully introduced against a very aggressive schedule.)

• In late 1998, Compaq Computer Corporation began a major initiative to sell their personal computers (PCs) directly to consumers, built to order. The company wanted to regain its place as the number one seller of PCs. Dell, an upstart at the time, had taken the top spot with a methodology that combined a sales force, phone orders, and Internet marketing. Their process was faster because it eliminated the middle seller. Furthermore, once an order was placed, Dell was able to build a computer in six hours. Compaq could not do that, and the difference was Dell's superb execution. Compaq simply could not perform as efficiently as Dell.

Eventually, Hewlett-Packard, another major PC-maker, acquired Compaq, and adding insult to Compaq's injury, the new combined behemoth suffered. HP kept shifting their goals, competing first on price, then on service. One solution was to fire CEO Carly Fiorina. Even without her at the helm, the company still was unsuccessful at execution.

• AT&T was once the world's biggest company, the world's biggest employer, and creator of the most advanced and reliable phone network that was the envy of industrialized countries. The company also put a reliable telephone in virtually every home in the U.S. But AT&T suffered a tragic fall. After the telecommunications industry was deregulated in 1982, AT&T lost its reason to exist. Facing competition from smaller providers that were once part of AT&T — the so-called "Baby Bells" — the company made a series of missteps. AT&T invested hundreds of billions of U.S. dollars into cable TV systems, cellular networks, local phone providers, long distance and global data networks — services in which the company was not competitive.

Management even split the company into four to provide services in cable TV, wireless phone, business services, and consumer services. But, the end came in January 2005. AT&T and SBC Communications announced an agreement whereby SBC would acquire AT&T to create the industry's premier communications and networking company. The company that had stood alone in the telecommunications world had become just another player because it could not find its footing in an altered marketplace.

What is significantly absent in the examples above is *leadership*:

Leadership in conveying a vision that was meaningful to others

Leadership in motivating teammates toward that vision

Leadership that is confident enough to share information on the progress of the project and foster cooperation, rather than withholding it to maintain personal control

Leadership in delegating assignments to people with the skill set and commitment required to get the job done

Leadership to help resolve interpersonal conflicts

Leadership in uncovering the hidden agendas that can stand in the way of success

Such barriers come in the form of the gatekeepers, those people several layers down from the CEO suites who are wary of the tried, true, and familiar. They prefer to maintain the status quo. These gatekeepers don't feel the need to implement a new piece of software that will help speed up processes. "We have gotten along without that for years. Why change now?"

Another reason for failure to execute is lack of measurement. It is shocking to learn how few companies actually follow up on their initiatives. (Marakon Associates estimates less than 15 percent). I know people who have survived at organizations for decades partly because they can guess which "programs of the month" require implementation and which are passing fads.

Below are two examples of seemingly ordinary people who faced difficult situations and ultimately triumphed over them with foresight, determination, and planning.

From Laggard to Leader

I once witnessed a wonderful example of ambitious goal setting, creative planning, and effective execution in the face of skepticism. But the most interesting part of this story for me is how the *employees* — not the management — refused to accept a change in their market, turning it back to their own advantage by conceiving an "impossible" goal, studying the needs of their market, and creating a strategy to meet that need with a newly redesigned product. They then implemented the design and won back a market that was all but lost.

My employer was a major industrial powerhouse that served companies around the world. At one time, they produced an air-cooled generator that was once one of the company's best products. However, over time, the generator lost its competitive edge. It took too much time to assemble and deliver. It was also technically inferior. Similar generators produced by other companies were more powerful, more reliable, and less expensive. In fact, some competitors were able to price this type of generator for less than this company could *make* it. So, management decided to outsource the generator; that is, find another lower-cost generator to sell under the company's name. In essence, they would concede this product and this market to the competition.

However, the employees were not ready simply to accept this plan. This generator was part of the company's history, and they did not want to be the people who doomed the product or surrendered the market to competitors without a fight. So the employees suggested that they put together a task force comprising engineers, marketers, and workers from the factory floor. Management agreed.

The marketers studied the customers' needs (amazingly, something they had not done previously). Their studies confirmed that customers based their purchase of an air-cooled generator on several factors. The team considered these selling points and planned how to respond to them:

- PERFORMANCE — The team determined to create a new design to meet the market's standards, as determined by megawatt output and other power ratings.

- DELIVERY — The generator's new design would lead to manufacturing procedures that would shorten the current delivery cycles without sacrificing market standards.

- COST — The new design would reduce costs by reducing the materials in it.

The manager of engineering likened his role to that of a coach on the sideline. "I got the right team on the field; they had to execute." The engineers asked hard questions that challenged the existing methodologies. They found alternatives that reduced the manufacturing cycle times and cut the cost of materials in half. They also began purchasing certain parts from the outside rather than making them internally, cutting costs by 30 percent.

Then the team examined manufacturing, discovering that some practices that were developed over time required extra people, resulting in extra time, extra costs, and longer manufacturing cycles. The general manager of the business told employees, "Our competitors are not more skilled than we are, nor are their facilities better. But their work force is more flexible. I don't want to lose business to another company simply because their people are working harder and smarter than ours are. And I don't think you do either." The manufacturing employees agreed to changes in their work practices.

The result was a generator that was re-engineered to require a lower number of parts, fewer welds, and less lamination (more cost savings), which resulted in a lighter weight. This was essentially a new product that was newly competitive, winning back business that was all but lost.

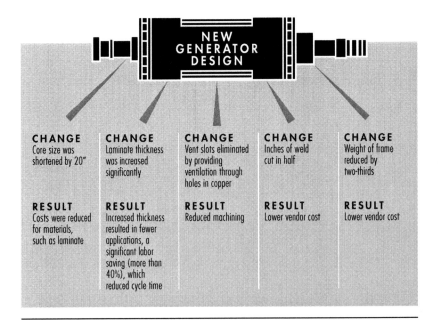

CHANGE	CHANGE	CHANGE	CHANGE	CHANGE
Core size was shortened by 20"	Laminate thickness was increased significantly	Vent slots eliminated by providing ventilation through holes in copper	Inches of weld cut in half	Weight of frame reduced by two-thirds
RESULT	RESULT	RESULT	RESULT	RESULT
Costs were reduced for materials, such as laminate	Increased thickness resulted in fewer applications, a significant labor saving (more than 40%), which reduced cycle time	Reduced machining	Lower vendor cost	Lower vendor cost

The team solved the problem by working the Six P's:

1. They **perceived** the changes in their market. Rather than rail against the changes, they accepted their circumstances as a reality and worked to resolve them.

2. They expanded their **perspective** of the market. They understood for the first time what their competitors had apparently learned much earlier: that cost and delivery times were critical to competitiveness. Rather than complain that the conditions were unfair, they adapted to them.

3. **Prognostication** — The team looked ahead and accurately predicted what it would take to succeed in the generator market.

4. The team **prepared proactively** and took control of their situation. They discussed the issues that affected their competitiveness, getting them all out in the open and exchanging solutions.

5. The team put this information together to create a **plan** of action. They listed the things that needed to be done and assigned responsibility for each tactic. What was very important was that they realized they had a deadline, as management needed to decide by a certain time whether they would outsource the air-cooled generator to another provider.

6. They **performed** superbly, executing the plan to its optimal benefit by fulfilling their individual responsibilities. The team also took the time to choose the right people to implement the tactics. The culture of the organization was better than they had given themselves credit for, and the details were carried out splendidly. Furthermore, the performances were measured to determine if they were proceeding successfully and on schedule. Engineers designed a more efficient generator that contained fewer parts, the purchasing department found the least expensive

suppliers of their parts, and the workers on the factory floor reviewed their methods to determine the most efficient ways to assemble the generator. And in the ultimate measurement, the product was validated by the marketplace, as it sold well and kept the company in the air-cooled generator market.

CHARTING A NEW COURSE

Joel Garblik learned that he liked the warmer weather of Florida when he visited the home of his dental school roommate. He kept that memory in the back of his mind, thinking that this could be a good place to practice one day. When he graduated from dental school, he took the dental board test there as well as in his hometown, just in case.

After Joel married his wife, Andie, the timing seemed right for a move. So the newlyweds relocated to Florida, and Joel grew both professionally and personally. He joined a group practice there as managing director. "I learned there was more to being a dentist than simply hanging a sign," he said. "I learned the business of dentistry." Over the next ten years, Joel and Andie gave birth to twin girls and a son. This was a time of which some young families can only dream.

But one day, Joel was driving on U.S. Route 19, cited by many as the most dangerous road in the entire United States. That morning, a large vehicle crossed several lanes to get to the median of the road. Joel was hidden from view by a very large truck, and his sports car was hit broadside. "It was the phone call you dread getting," said Andie, remembering how she learned that Joel was in the emergency room for observation. The good news was that he was released the next day, but this was just the beginning of his situation. Worse news was yet to come.

Joel knew within hours of the accident that he couldn't use his hands. The impact had damaged several of the vertebrae in his neck, which in turn affected his ulnar nerve, a main nerve in the arm. When we injure this nerve in our day-to-day lives, we commonly call it "hitting the funny bone." Here there was no joke, as Joel described the sensation as "profoundly numb, as though my hand has fallen asleep." Without the ability to handle dental tools and perform fine procedures, Joel's career as a dentist was over.

Luckily for his family, Joel had top-notch disability insurance. He even had the foresight to add a valuable rider that allowed him to retire at a livable income. But the comfort of financial stability was not enough for Joel. He needed to find some other way to make a living and be productive. But how, when his main craft was suddenly taken from him?

Even while his dental practice was successful, Joel and a neighbor were dabbling with computers as a hobby. Joel's friend, who was a corporate engineer, was working with a then-unique practice: electronic billing for physicians. In those days, such office computerization was just beginning. Joel's friend would collect paperwork from doctors' offices, keypunch the data and electronically transfer it to the insurance company for reimbursement.

Joel thought that this was a good way to occupy his time from 9 to 5 since he could no longer work as a dentist. Because he had served as office manager for the dental practice, he understood reimbursement practices. So Joel and his friends started a company that they named National Computer Claims Services (NCCS). He could help his fellow dentists in the area obtain their reimbursements for a small fee per transaction. There wasn't much money in it — Joel called it "beer money" — but he was living off his disability income anyway. For now, the work was something to do with his time. More importantly, it was something new to learn.

Even though the company grew, it still wasn't very big. "We were too big to be small yet too small to be big," he recalls, but Joel and his partners continued to develop the business. Six years after dabbling in physician reimbursement, their company was purchased by ENVOY Corporation, a major provider of electronic payment services to the healthcare industry. Joel and company not only received cash to pay off their business-related debts, but they became employees of ENVOY. Joel received a four-year contract to serve as vice president of marketing for electronic claims. So throughout the course of their contracts, Joel and his NCCS partners were helping to run their company as a wholly owned subsidiary of ENVOY.

An added bonus was that the new position allowed Joel, Andie, and their children to return to their hometown, as they had become homesick.

Joel realized over time that, although he was treated well by ENVOY, he was not suited to a corporate bureaucracy. When his contracted expired, he left on friendly terms, but he had no idea what he would do next.

During his time with ENVOY, Joel had developed a friendly rivalry with Joseph, another dentist who was running a similar reimbursement processing company. (The two often referred work to each other, despite the fact that they were supposedly competing.) Joseph invited Joel to be part of his company after the contract with ENVOY ended, and the two men enjoyed what Joel described as a "wonderful relationship" for seven more years. Joel's and Joseph's work together ended when Joseph's company was purchased by a major medical internet company (which, coincidentally, had purchased ENVOY in the interim). So Joel found himself as a corporate employee again. In fact, he was essentially employed by the same corporation! Joel and this new conglomerate parted amicably again after two years. Today, though only in his 50s, Joel is comfortably retired.

That could have been the end of Joel's story. In many ways, it has a happy ending, as his physical condition has since improved, with the numbing sensation limited to his left side. But Joel has not been content with retirement, so he began looking again for a meaningful occupation. Some time ago, he saw an ad by a local medical school for a graduate program in forensic medicine. When he was studying dentistry, he had been interested in the discipline of "forensic odontology," a branch of investigative medicine that deals with the proper examination, handling, and presentation of dental evidence in a court of law. This program was an extension of that activity, so he applied for it. Joel is pursuing his classes now, and when he is finished, he will have a Master of Science in forensic medicine and the start of yet another new career.

Looking back, Joel says he is only slightly disappointed that he did not remain a dentist. "I invested four years of education and a good deal of money into learning," he says. "I studied for the boards, and we relocated to Florida. So on a ten-point scale, my disappointment is about a six. But everything turned out well."

Joel explains why he was not crushed by his sudden turn in fortune as others may have been. "I never believed you need to be brilliant or financially supported to succeed in life; you only need to be motivated and confident enough to tackle a new challenge," he says. "You must also be able to envision what you can do day-to-day. I understood that, as a dentist, I had more in me than the motor skills to handle a drill and instruments. I also had these cognitive skills that I could put to work in a business."

Joel overcame his unexpected challenges by envisioning himself as "Joel Garblik, Incorporated," and then by following the Six P's:

1. He **perceived** that it was possible to undergo changes to his vocation and still support his family and his lifestyle. He prepared for that possibility by funding a very strong disability policy.

2. Though clearly shocked by this sudden change in their lives, Joel and Andie maintained a healthy **perspective** of their situations. They both understood that Joel was not totally incapacitated by his injury and that he could find another way to make a living.

3. Joel took his knowledge of the evolving practice of medicine and **prognosticated** that changes were coming to the reimbursement of dentists and other physicians. He identified ways to serve those upcoming needs.

4. Joel **prepared proactively** for the development of "Joel Garblik, Incorporated" by learning new computer skills and practicing them diligently around the clock.

5. Joel and his friends put together a **plan** with measurable goals. Together, they sought to achieve a certain dollar number of billings every month, and then they put that little bit of cash back into the business to grow it.

6. Joel and his partners **performed**, meeting the modest objectives of their plan until they were purchased by a bigger entity. With new corporate resources at their disposal, they grew the company, serving more customers in a wider number of markets.

I look forward to learning how "Joel Garblik, Incorporated" expands his mission by applying his forensics degree to the next chapter of his life. He has proven himself an able change agent rather than a victim of his circumstances.

These stories serve as examples of how people who are buffeted by seemingly unstoppable change can exert some control over their situations. The system works, when you work the system!

Lessons from Step 6

1. While it's important to be able to visualize the future and plan for it, as a change agent you must also develop your performance (i.e., the execution of your plan). It is a skill often overlooked because others often delegate execution to others. Luckily, you have the ability to develop your own performance abilities.

2. Successful implementation depends on the following elements:

   a. Leadership

   b. Teamwork

   c. Communication

   d. Managing interpersonal conflicts

   e. Uncovering hidden agendas

   Make sure these elements exist for you, wherever applicable.

3. The shortage of skills in execution can have serious consequences in the change process. One may envision the future, predict it, prepare for it, and develop a plan to deal with it. Yet that person may be unable to implement the final strategy.

4. Measurement is important to judging the success of execution. In short, you must ask yourself, "Did I do what I set out to do?" History is littered with grand plans that were never realized.

Intermission For Your Transition

Let's Make it Happen!

1. You are now ready to implement the plan that you have devised to manage the changes and transitions that you face. This is an opportunity to pat yourself on the back; list your skills that will help you accomplish your goals. *(Examples include leadership, organization skills, or your resourcefulness. Don't let these examples limit your thinking. Let loose with all that you can do that will help you meet change head on.)*

_____

_____

_____

_____

_____

_____

_____

2. Anticipate the barriers that may stand in the way of your implementation. Brainstorm them, considering all possibilities.

_____

_____

_____

_____

_____

_____

3. Now that you are aware of the things that may stand in your way, how will you overcome them? _(For example, you may uncover hidden agendas by holding open forums with the parties who may have a stake in your project. You may choose to purchase a skill that you don't have yourself, ranging anywhere from a certified public accountant to a painter for that new room you are redesigning. Again, just let your thoughts fly and pour through your pen and paper.)_

_____

_____

_____

_____

_____

4. **How have your efforts stacked up against your success measurements? Did you succeed?** *(Refer back to the "measurable goals" that we discussed earlier.)*

_____

_____

_____

_____

_____

_____

And Now is the Time to Implement The Six P's of Change

Change is with us continually, even persistently. Look at our lives. We are in transition from the moment we are roused from the dark and peaceful slumber of our mothers' wombs by a stranger who pulls us into the light of a new world. Change has many qualities. It is remarkable. It is mundane. It is frightful. It is exhilarating. We love it when we think it's good, when it comes as a renewal. But we resent it when we regard it as regenerative. But whichever change we experience, it is important to remember that these transitions are with us during all our days on this Earth, from that first change that occurs at birth until that final change.

Many people hate change. That disdain usually springs from the inability to deal with change. But when the trail through transformation becomes clear, then people are better able to accept it, often regarding it as an opportunity for renewal. That is why those of us who are leading change must recognize the adventure in it. As leaders, we must communicate that sense of exploration and wonder. Look at how exciting it can be! Change can lead us to a place where we would not ordinarily go, whether it is a new relationship, a new line of work, or a new place to live.

Yet change may also cause us to surrender something, whether it is a possession, a person, or a proudly held position. This relinquishing of some part of our past, however small, can be painful. We can feel lost and dissonant until we right ourselves again. Only then can we begin again.

Beginning again in the face of transition is the purpose of the Six P's — to help remove the ambiguities that often come with change, teaching us to handle them more effectively and more easily. As we undergo our transitions — our movements from one situation to the next — we must learn to handle them smoothly and gracefully. To be sure, many of us are better equipped to deal with change than others may be. There are people in this world who have personal qualities that make them more naturally optimistic. Those of us who don't possess that natural inclination must learn to optimize our unique and individual abilities in order to adapt to a shifting environment. We must learn to be the best "change agent" we are *capable* of being. It would be disingenuous of me to claim that I have always been able to handle the diversions in my own journey. While I met some challenges with skill and grace, I must also admit that others set me back financially, physically, emotionally, and even spiritually. I once experienced a bout of depression after a seemingly non-stop period of problems and challenges. Even still, that was a lesson for me, as I discovered my boundaries and learned to act within them. I learned to ask the right questions both of myself and my situations, and I learned to seek the most appropriate answers. This newfound knowledge was truly liberating.

So let's end this book as we began it — with a baseball analogy. When life hits a ground ball between your legs, can you field it for an out? Or, will it instead set off a chain of events that enriches someone else while you are left on the sidelines?

I believe that YOU can be the winner if you follow the steps that we have laid out:

1) Develop the **Perception** that change is a reality.

2) Gain the **Perspective** that change is often neither all positive nor all negative.

3) Learn the art of **Prognostication**, which is all about predicting the future the best you can before it happens to you.

4) Practice **Proactive Preparation** for whatever you envision down the road. Or even those situations that you can't foresee.

5) Develop **Planning** — a step-by-step strategy that will meet your defined goals.

6) Implement **Performance** of your plan, executing all of it superbly.

As you move forward in your goals, whatever they may be, I know that you will face changes, and most of them will enhance your life. So I will not wish you protection from such opportunities. Quite to the contrary, I wish you a *change-filled* life —

Change that will make you happy…

Change that will make you feel fulfilled…

But most important, change that **you** will make.

NOTES

Nearly all of the incidents and anecdotes in this book to illustrate my points are based on my first-hand experiences. Others were the result of secondary research derived from a variety of sources, including books, periodicals and the Internet. In most cases, I referenced the source of the information in my text. My intention here is to acknowledge, to the best of my ability, and with gratitude, the other writers and researchers whose work enriched this book. I also wish to refer you to their publications in order that you may further expand your knowledge of historical change.

Step 2 — P E R S P E C T I V E

p. 40 There is an apocryphal story that says that Edison's son, Charles, found his father watching the fire, and that the elder Edison shouted, "Charles, where's your mother? Find her. Bring her here. She will never see anything like this as long as she lives." The story goes on to state that on the next day, Edison surveyed the charred remnants of his facility and said, "There is great value in disaster. All our mistakes are burned up. Thank God we can start anew." Then, it is said, Edison delivered the first phonograph a few weeks later.

Not only could I not find evidence of this story in any reputable source, but also history records that Edison had invented the phonograph prior to the 1914 fire in New Jersey. However, the version of the story of the West Orange fire cited in this book is documented in Robert Conot's well-regarded biography of Edison, "*A Streak of Luck*," published by Seaview Books, March 1979.

p. 47 The information about Louis Braille was inspired by a segment in "*More of the Rest of the Story*," by Paul Harvey, published by Bantam Books, July 1984. It was supplemented by general biographical information in the Encyclopedia Britannica.

p. 47-48 The biographies of Anthony Burgess and J.K. Rowling were both adapted from information found on Wikipedia.

Step 3 — PROGNOSTICATION

p. 55 The description of King Gillette's development of the safety razor appeared in the November 22, 1999 edition of *Fortune* magazine as part of an article titled "*Products of the Century*" by Christine Chen and Tim Carvell. The article chronicled the best products of the 20th century.

p. 56 The description of how New York Governor DeWitt Clinton funded and built the Erie Canal appeared as part of an article, "*10 Moments That Made American Business*," by John Steele Gordon, which was published in *American Heritage* magazine, February/March 2007.

p. 57 Much of the biographical information about H. G. Wells first appeared in "*Discovering the Future*," by Paul Crabtree, an article published in the May-June 2008 issue of *The Futurist* magazine. It was also supplemented by information found on Wikipedia.

Step 4 — PROACTIVE PREPARATION

p. 90 The information about Charles M. (Chuck) Geschke and John Warnock, the founders of Adobe Systems, was first published in an interview with Mr. Geschke that appeared in the September 03, 2008 edition of the Knowledge@Wharton newsletter, published by the Wharton School of Business of the University of Pennsylvania.

Step 5 — PLANNING

p. 107 The story of Mr. Tony Bennett's career has been documented in a variety of publications, including Wikipedia and in *AARP* magazine ("*Tony Bennett*" by John Lewis in the July-August 2003 issue). However, the original and most reliable source of this information is Mr. Bennett's autobiography, "*The Good Life*," published by Pocket Books in 1998.

Pat Rocchi is a versatile communicator — speaker, author, media producer, and consultant — with many years of experience in a wide variety of industries, such as healthcare, information technology, and manufacturing. As a communications and marketing leader who is both an MBA and a Master of Education, Pat is a proven leader of positive change. He has earned awards from many organizations, including Toastmasters International in PA and NJ, the International Association of Business Communicators, the International Mercury Award, and the NY International Film and TV Festival. While Pat was employed by General Electric, he won the company's top communication award four times. He has also worked in a wide variety of media, including the Web, video and film, and print.

Contact Pat at patrocchi@comcast.net to share your ideas about *"The Six P's of Change,"* and other communication matters. He is also available as a keynote speaker, educational seminar leader, and as a consultant in speechwriting and coaching, marketing, external communication and media production.